SBD
DAUNTLESS

A DETAIL & SCALE AVIATION PUBLICATION

in detail & scale

Bert Kinzey

squadron/signal publications

COPYRIGHT © 1996 BY DETAIL & SCALE, INC.

This book is a product of Detail & Scale, Inc., which has sole responsibility for its content and layout, except that all contributors are responsible for the security clearance and copyright release of all materials submitted. Published by Squadron/Signal Publications, 1115 Crowley Drive, Carrollton, Texas 75011. ISBN 1-888974-01-X

CONTRIBUTORS AND SOURCES:

Jeff Ethell
Lloyd Jones
Dana Bell
Clyde Mills
Jim Galloway

Jim Roeder
J. C. Bahr
Keith Liles
Low Pass, Inc.
Confederate Air Force

National Archives
National Museum of Naval Aviation
USS YORKTOWN Museum
U. S. Marine Corps Museum
U. S. Air Force Museum

Planes of Fame Museum
National Air & Space Museum
U. S. Navy
U. S. Marine Corps
U. S. Air Force

Many photographs in this publication are credited to their contributors. Photographs with no credit indicated were taken by the author.

The author expresses a sincere word of thanks to Jeff Ethell. On very short notice, Jeff provided many of the color photographs in this book, including the one on the front cover.

A special word of thanks is also extended to John Neel and all of the Low Pass crew who so beautifully and authentically restored SBD-3, 06508. The reason that so many accurate detailed photographs are included in this book is because Casey Hill, a member of the Low Pass crew, invited the author to photograph this Dauntless during the entire restoration process.

Another "thank you" is deserved by "Tex" Layton of the Confederate Air Force who invited the author to photograph the restoration of the Dixie Wing's SBD-5. "Tex" also loaned the author seven different Douglas, Navy, and Army manuals on the Dauntless and the Banshee during the preparation of this book, and these manuals provided invaluable information on the physical features of the aircraft.

Finally, the author would like to thank Ludlow Porch, the world's most entertaining radio talk show host, for permitting the author to make an appeal for a microfilm reader over Ludlow's Funseekers' Network. The reader that was found allowed members of the Confederate Air Force to study many rolls of microfilm about the Dauntless during the restoration of their aircraft. In this way, Ludlow not only significantly helped return a bit of aviation history to flying status, he also helped indirectly with the preparation of this book.

Above (Front cover photo): This excellent photograph of an SBD-3 was taken during the second half of 1942, and it illustrates the blue-gray over light gray paint scheme to good effect. The markings reflect those used after all red was ordered removed from aircraft on 20 May, 1942. This order eliminated the red disc at the center of the national insignia and the red and white stripes from the rudder. The effects of weathering on the paint can easily be studied in this large photograph. The colors of the uniforms worn by the pilot, gunner, and flight deck crew are also shown in this picture. (U. S. Navy photo via Ethell)

Right (Rear cover photo): Colors and details of the pilot's instrument panel in an SBD-3 are revealed in this photograph.

INTRODUCTION

The Dauntless was an all-metal monoplane with low-mounted wings, a single radial engine, and a retractable main landing gear. But it shared these design features with many other military aircraft of its day including the SNJ trainer and the F6F Hellcat. Indeed, there was nothing uniquely outstanding about its design, however its simple but proven features and its rugged construction combined to make it an effective combat aircraft when it was most needed. Pilots reported that it had very similar flying characteristics to the SNJ, and because of their nimble handling qualities, Dauntlesses sometimes flew combat air patrol missions where they more than held their own against Japanese carrier-based aircraft. (National Archives)

SBD; in official Navy terminology these letters stand for Scout-Bomber, Douglas, denoting both the aircraft's type and its builder. But during World War II, the words **S**low **B**ut **D**eadly were more often associated with the designation for the Dauntless scout and dive bomber. Already considered obsolete by the Navy when Pearl Harbor was attacked, the Dauntless remained in action throughout the war, in part because of problems encountered with its replacement, the Curtiss SB2C Helldiver. But even after the Helldiver replaced the Dauntless in front line squadrons, it did not replace it in the hearts of its crews. The Dauntless, although slow and lacking sufficient defensive armament, was loved by the men who flew and serviced it. By comparison, the Helldiver was nicknamed the "Beast" and continued to have problems throughout its operational career.

This volume is the first of the Detail & Scale Series in several years to feature an aircraft from World War II. The lack of World War II titles is not because of preference, but is due to the format of the Detail & Scale Series. This series focuses on the many physical details of each aircraft, so numerous photographs of its features, both inside and out, are required. Unfortunately, this type of photograph is not commonly found in the National Archives or other sources. Manufacturers of World War II aircraft had files of detailed photographs at one time, but very few of these companies remain in business today.

Without extensive photographic files available that show details, the only other way to illustrate the aircraft in detail is to shoot new photographs. Regrettably, many "restored" aircraft that are now in museums are nothing more than shells, having been gutted of their cockpit equipment, armament, and sometimes even their engines. Those that have been restored to flying status no longer appear as they did when they waged combat more than fifty years ago. Modern requirements have necessitated the addition of radio and navigation equipment that did not even exist when the aircraft was operational with the

military. New antennas sprout from the aircraft where before there were none. More often than not, the paint schemes are only loosely based on the warpaint formerly worn by the aircraft, or at least one of its variants. The paint is usually glossy for ease of maintenance instead of having the correct flat finish. In most cases then, restored World War II aircraft, both flying and static, do not usually offer an acceptable alternative to finding vintage detailed photographs of the aircraft as it appeared in service.

Fortunately, because of the fiftieth anniversary of World War II, more aircraft are being restored, and an added emphasis has been placed on authenticity. This is true for both flying and static restorations, and the Dauntless is one case in point. Less than twenty miles from Detail & Scale's office, the Confederate Air Force is restoring its A-24B, 42-54532, to flying condition. It will be rebuilt to SBD-5 standards and painted in markings appropriate for that variant. Formerly, the CAF had operated this aircraft in SBD-3 markings. After removing every piece of equipment, the CAF is rebuilding it with extensive attention to detail. When fully restored, there will be only one or two extra whip antennas, and the modern radios will be concealed to as great an extent as possible. This Dauntless promises to become one of the most extensively detailed and historically accurate aircraft in the CAF's inventory.

Just a stone's throw down the road from where the CAF is rebuilding its A-24B, an SBD-3 has recently been restored in meticulous detail by John Neel and his Low Pass crew at the Georgia Metal Shaping Company. No detail was overlooked as this SBD-3 was returned to the condition it was in when it flew with both the Marines and the Navy during World War II. It was the restoration of this aircraft that made this book possible. Because the various versions of the Dauntless differed very little in physical detail, shooting extensive photographs of this SBD-3 provided almost complete coverage of the famous dive bomber's details. Photographs of those features that did change between one variant and another were obtained from the National Archives, Navy files, private collections, and through photography of other restored aircraft where the features were authentically represented. In all, detailed photographs were taken of seven restored SBDs and A-24s.

Dozens of detailed photographs taken during the restoration of SBD-3, BuNo. 06508, appear in this book. It is therefore appropriate to review its varied and historic past in this introduction.

SBD-3, 06508, was accepted by the U. S. Navy from the Douglas Aircraft factory at El Segundo, California, on 17 July, 1942. It was received by the Pacific Fleet Aircraft Pool at NAS North Island the following day and made ready for shipment to the Pacific Theater. On 22 July, it left California by surface vessel and arrived at Pearl Harbor on 15 August where it was received by Carrier Aircraft Service Unit One (CASU-1) for further transfer to Pacific fleet units. On 15 September, it was placed on the deck of the USS COPAHEE, AVC-12 at Pearl Harbor. Then on 28 September, after the COPAHEE had finished loading her cargo of replacement aircraft, pilots, crewmen, and aviation stores, the ship departed for Noumea, New Caledonia.

On 11 November, the aircraft was received by Marine Scouting-Bomber Squadron 141 (VMSB-141), becoming part of the Cactus Air Force at Henderson Field on Guadalcanal. But VMSB-141 departed from Guadalcanal eight days later, and 06508 was transferred to VMSB-132. While serving with these two Marine squadrons, the Dauntless saw extensive combat service including missions up "The Slot" to attack Japanese shipping. On several occasions, the Dauntless was hit by enemy fire as verified by the holes and patches that were still in its airframe and skin when restoration began fifty years later.

The SBD-3 was turned over to the Marine Service Squadron in Marine Air Group 11 at Esprito Santos for service and repair on 15 February, 1943. It was then reassigned to U. S. Navy Bombing Squadron 10 (VB-10) as a replacement aircraft. At that time, VB-10 was part of the air wing embarked in USS ENTERPRISE, CV-6. The aircraft's log book shows that this transfer took place on 23 March, 1943. However, 06508 did not fly from the "Big E's" decks very long, because the famous carrier soon returned to the United States for a yard period. On 1 May, ENTERPRISE departed the New Hebrides with SBD-3, 06508, still aboard, and the carrier headed for Hawaii enroute to the United States. On 8 May, VB-10 flew ashore to Ford Island. From there the SBD-3 was shipped back to NAS Alameda, California.

The veteran Dauntless was repaired at NAS North Island, then reassigned to the Carrier Qualification Training Unit at NAS Glenview, Illinois, on 2 October. On 23 November, 06508 was flown by Ensign Edward E. Hendrickson, USNR, for the purpose of making his initial carrier qualification landings aboard the training carrier USS WOLVERINE. On his third attempt, Hendrickson received the "cut" signal from the LSO, but he was slightly to the port side of the deck. Upon contact with the ship, he hit the port catwalk. The Dauntless continued on over the port side in an inverted position, then it sank in Lake Michigan after remaining afloat for about one minute. Hendrickson survived the accident, but 06508 remained under water for forty-seven years before being recovered.

The author was informed about the restoration of 06508 by Casey Hill, a member of John Neel's crew. During the months of restoration and at its delivery to the National Museum of Naval Aviation, the author took hundreds of photographs of 06508's details.

In order to illustrate as many details as possible, the historical summary has been kept to a minimum. For those interested in a more in-depth look at the SBD's operational record, Detail & Scale recommends Barrett Tillman's The Dauntless Dive Bomber of World War II. This excellent publication was first released by the Naval Institute Press in 1976.

The purpose of this new volume in the Detail & Scale Series is to illustrate and describe the physical features of the Dauntless in greater detail than any other publication available to the general public. We have also included our usual Modelers Section with reviews of kits, accessories, and decals available to the scale modeler.

Detail & Scale thanks John Neel and his crew for the opportunity to photograph 06508 in detail on numerous occasions. Thanks also go to Tex Layton of the Confederate Air Force for helping with photography of the aircraft under restoration by the CAF. Tex loaned seven different SBD manuals to the author during the preparation of this book. Several drawings were taken from these manuals for use in this publication, and the manuals were also used to insure accuracy in writing the captions for the photographs. Finally, a special word of thanks goes to Casey Hill for encouraging the author to produce this book on the **S**low **B**ut **D**eadly Dauntless.

The Low Pass crew poses with Robert L. Rasmussen, Director of the National Museum of Naval Aviation, as SBD-3, 06508, is delivered to the museum in March 1994. Reclining is Renee Hurt. Kneeling from left to right are Casey Hill, Stacy Martin, Michelle Jackson, and Bill Hardin. Standing from left to right are Robert Rasmussen, John Neel, Jonas Josselson, Randy Jackson, and Joe Bekardesco. Sam Knob, who painted the Dauntless, is not pictured.

HISTORICAL SUMMARY

The design for the Dauntless can be traced back to Northrop's XBT-1, which also featured perforated dive flaps.
(National Archives)

In 1934, the U. S. Navy approached aircraft manufacturers with specifications for a new plane that was intended to serve both as a scout and a dive bomber. Six manufacturers responded with proposals, but the two from Curtiss and Great Lakes were quickly eliminated because they were bi-planes. The Navy had decided that the all-metal monoplane was the way to go.

The remaining four designs came from Brewster, Martin, Northrop, and Vought. Of these, the proposals from Northrop and Vought were selected for further development. Vought's design would result in the limited production of the SB2U Vindicator, but it was Northrop's XBT-1 which offered more potential as a dive bomber. Heading up the design team was Ed Heinemann who was instrumental in the design of a number of famous naval

aircraft for many years.

The XBT-1 began flight testing in December 1935, and in early 1936 an order for fifty-four production BT-1s was placed by the Navy. Although these aircraft did serve with squadrons aboard USS YORKTOWN (CV-5) and USS ENTERPRISE (CV-6), the Navy was less than satisfied with its performance. The problem centered primarily around the 825-horsepower Pratt & Whitney engine. To correct these shortcomings, work began on the XBT-2 to which a more powerful Wright XR-1820-32 engine with a three-blade propeller was fitted. The design was refined to reduce drag, and the large landing gear fairings of the BT-1 were eliminated in favor of a fully retractable main gear. Considerable attention was also given to the design of the ailerons and tail surfaces.

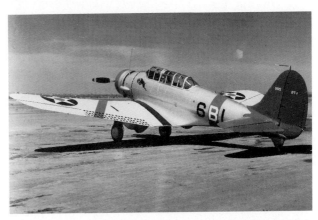

The production BT-1 shared many features with the subsequent Dauntless. These two photos show the aircraft that was assigned to the squadron commander of Bombing Six aboard the USS ENTERPRISE (CV-6). Like on the XBT-1, the landing gear of the BT-1 folded back into large fairings under the swings, and this proved less than satisfactory.
(National Archives)

Refinements to the design of the BT-1 are illustrated in this photograph of the XBT-2 which was the prototype for the Dauntless. Most visible of these are the fully retractable main landing gear, the shape of the cowling, and the design of the vertical tail and rudder. However, what made the new design a success was the increase in power provided by the XR-1820-32 engine which produced 1,000 horsepower. (National Archives)

When Jack Northrop started his company in El Segundo, California, in 1932, he maintained close ties with Douglas Aircraft, so when Northrop left El Segundo in early 1938, Douglas took over the plant and the development of the XBT-2. Accordingly, the designation was changed to XSBD-1 by the Navy. This reflected not only the scout bomber mission of the aircraft, but the D designator for Douglas replaced the T used for Northrop.

In April 1939, orders were placed for fifty-seven SBD-1s for the Marines and eighty-seven SBD-2s for the Navy. These first two variants differed mainly with respect to the amount of fuel carried. The first operational SBD-1s were assigned to Marine squadrons VMB-2 and VMB-1 in late 1940 and early 1941 respectively. These units were subsequently redesignated VMSB-232 and VMSB-132 prior to the attack on Pearl Harbor. Initial deliveries of SBD-2s went to VB-6, VS-6, VB-2 and VS-2.

The SBD-3 began to come off the production line in

The first production version of the Dauntless was the SBD-1. All examples of this variant were given to the Marines, and this was the only version of the Dauntless to be painted in a colorful pre-war paint scheme. The bands on the cowling and aft fuselage are red, as are the stripes on the wing. The vertical stripes on the rudder are red, white, and blue, beginning with the trailing edge and moving forward. The fuselage, the tail surfaces (except for the rudder) and the underside of the wings are silver. The tops of the wings are yellow. The national insignia has the red disc in the center and is on all four wing positions. However, there are no national insignias on the fuselage.

(National Archives)

A rear seat gunner in an SBD-3 snapped this shot of other Dauntlesses as they warmed up their engines in preparation for a raid in early 1942. The small white cowl numbers have been overpainted with larger black ones, but the large national insignias and rudder stripes are in evidence. The aircraft closest to the camera has a spinner, while the others do not. Note the bombs in place under the fuselage of each aircraft. (National Archives)

March 1941. It was primarily this variant that fought the crucial battles of 1942, turning back the Japanese invasion force at Coral Sea and sinking four enemy carriers at the Battle of Midway. Other Navy and Marine SBD-3s operated from carriers and from Henderson Field during the desparate battle for Guadalcanal and the Eastern Solomons later that year.

Dauntlesses saw their first combat action when several SBDs from VS-6 and VB-6 aboard USS ENTERPRISE arrived over Pearl Harbor during the Japanese attack on 7 December, 1941. Two Japanese aircraft were shot down by the SBDs, but overall the Japanese came out on top. Several Dauntlesses were shot down or forced to crash land, while Marine SBD-1s were destroyed or damaged on the ground during the attack. Some measure of revenge was gained on 10 December when an SBD-2, piloted by Lieutenant Clarence Dickinson from ENTERPRISE, sank the Japanese submarine I-70. With this sinking, the Dauntless became the first American aircraft to sink a Japanese ship during World War II. Having been operational when the Japanese attacked Pearl Harbor and also at the time of their surrender in 1945, the Dauntless shares with the Wildcat the distinction of being one of only two U. S. Navy carrier-based aircraft to be in continu-

ous operation throughout the entire U. S. involvement in the war in the Pacific.

Although the Dauntless served admirably throughout the entire war in the Pacific, it was during the desperate battles of 1942 where the importance of its contributions cannot be overstated and where it achieved its most significant successes.

After raids on Kwajalein, Rabaul, Wake Island, Marcus Island, Lae, and Salamaua, American carriers participated in more dramatic and important actions. During Dolittle's B-25 strike against Japan, SBDs from ENTERPRISE flew scouting missions around the task force but were not directly involved in combat. However, things were far different further to the south.

While ENTERPRISE and HORNET (CV-8) were returning from the Dolittle raid, LEXINGTON (CV-2) and YORKTOWN (CV-5) were sent south to the Coral Sea to defend against a Japanese thrust toward Australia. The first action by American carrier forces in the Battle of Coral Sea consisted of two attacks on Tulagi by YORKTOWN's planes. Among them were SBDs from VB-5 and VS-5. These attacks occurred on 4 May, 1942, and while some limited successes were achieved, they were only a small prelude to what would happen three days later.

Up until 7 May, the Battle of Coral Sea had been very similar to the revenge raids that had taken place against Japanese shore installations earlier in the year. Although enemy shipping had been attacked in harbors, there had been no major engagement between the American and Japanese fleets. But this was all about to change, and the SBDs were going to play the major role.

Early in the morning of 7 May, Dauntlesses were launched to look for the Japanese naval units that were known to be in the area. Shortly after 0730 that morning, one SBD spotted two enemy cruisers, while two others shot down Japanese floatplanes. It was obvious that the Japanese were close by.

About half-an-hour later, another Dauntless pilot discovered what he reported as two Japanese aircraft carriers with several escorting ships northwest of the American force. Rear Admiral Jack Fletcher, the American commander, continued to close the distance between his ships and the Japanese, then he launched his strike just before 0930. Wildcats, Devastators, and Dauntlesses roared off of LEXINGTON (CV-2) and YORKTOWN to strike the Japanese. Over half of these planes were SBDs.

In the meantime, the scouts began to return, and it was discovered that the earlier report about the two carriers had been in error. The sighting had been of two cruisers instead. With this corrected information, and a new report from an Army B-17 which had sighted a Japanese carrier, Fletcher had a more accurate idea about the enemy's disposition. The information was radioed to the strike force which was now getting close to the reported Japanese position.

It wasn't long before the wakes of the enemy ships were visible in the water, and the American aircraft turned toward their targets. They had found the Japanese invasion force with its transports and the light carrier SHOHO that was providing air cover. SHOHO was the primary target as the planes lined up to attack.

At about the same time as the first Dauntlesses began to attack, Zero fighters from SHOHO started to make firing passes at the Americans, but one by one the SBDs pushed over into their dives on the targets below. Perhaps the best known Dauntless of all time, 2-S-12 from VS-2, was being flown by Ensign John Leppla. In the rear cockpit was Airman Third Class John Liska. As they approached the push-over point, Liska claimed two Zeros with his single .30-caliber machine gun, while Leppla dispatched another during the dive with his twin .50s.

After LEXINGTON's SBDs had dropped their bombs and scored several direct hits and near misses, VT-2's Devastators came in with their torpedoes and did more damage to the stricken carrier. Next came YORKTOWN's SBDs, and finally VT-5's torpedo planes. Meanwhile, LCDR Bob Dixon, who had led a group of SBDs from LEXINGTON, watched the attack from high above the action after dropping his own bomb. As SHOHO disappeared under the waves, Dixon radioed one of the most famous reports in naval aviation history, "Scratch one flattop!"

But the SBD's were still not finished. On his way back to LEXINGTON, Leppla shot down a floatplane. More importantly, with SHOHO sunk, the transports heading for the invasion of Port Moresby turned around, thus ending that threat against Australia. But the American's suffered losses on 7 May as well. Japanese carrier-based aircraft sank the destroyer SIMS and the oiler NEOSHO.

There were still two large Japanese carriers known to be in the area, so the next morning Fletcher launched SBDs to seek them out. It was almost 0830 when the enemy carriers and their escorts were sighted, and a strike was launched at near maximum range. Although foul weather caused some aircraft in the strike force to return without ever finding the enemy, others did find ZUIKAKU and SHOKAKU in between the rain squalls and clouds. Of those that did attack, the only ones to score hits were SBDs which severely damaged SHOKAKU.

Meanwhile, Japanese planes had found the American ships, and LEXINGTON was hit and mortally wounded. Internal explosions ultimately doomed the carrier, and she sank with many of her aircraft still on board. YORKTOWN was also damaged, but not severely enough to cause her to sink. Again Dauntlesses made their presence known in defense of the American ships. Flying an inner ring of combat air patrol, SBDs shot down at least five Japanese torpedo planes and dive bombers. Many others were damaged or had to abort their attacks against the two American carriers and their escorts.

The Battle of Coral Sea became the first engagement between two opposing naval surface forces that fought the battle without the ships of one side coming in visual range of the other. It was fought entirely by aircraft, and one carrier on each side was lost. While the loss of a fleet carrier by the Americans, as well as the sinking of the SIMS and NEOSHO, might seem to outweigh the loss of the small SHOHO, the invasion of Australia was stopped, and this made the battle a strategic success in favor of the Americans. Throughout the historic battle, SBDs had played a major role on both offense and defense.

One shortcoming of the Dauntless had been noted during the Battle of Coral Sea, and that was the inadequate defensive firepower of the single flexible machine gun. An urgent message was submitted requesting a change to a dual .30-caliber mount, and this modification was made to existing SBD-3s almost immediately.

What many historians would claim to be the most significant battle in naval history would take place less than a month after the final shots were fired in the Coral Sea. The Japanese move to take Midway had been discovered through the brilliant code-breaking work of Naval Intelligence, and Admiral Chester Nimitz was as ready as the forces at his disposal allowed him to be. After hasty repairs were made to patch up the damage received by YORKTOWN during the Battle of Coral Sea, she joined ENTERPRISE and HORNET at Point Luck northeast of Midway to await the Japanese. Aboard the three carriers were over one hundred Dauntlesses, almost all of which were SBD-3s. A few SBD-2s were also present aboard HORNET. Additionally, a handful of SBD-2s were assigned to VMSB-241 of Marine Air Group 22 on Midway. These Marine aircraft were the first to attack Admiral Nagumo's carrier striking force, but they scored no hits against the Japanese ships. Their counterparts in the Navy were to have much better success.

If the Battle of Midway proved nothing else, it was that skill, bravery, sacrifice, and luck all played important roles in determining the victor in combat. When the Japanese carrier force of AKAGI, KAGA, SORYU, and

HIRYU were sighted, the American carriers launched their aircraft at maximum range. Separated and disoriented, the American squadrons attacked individually and without mutual support if and when they found the Japanese. Torpedo squadrons came in first, drawing the enemy's fighters down low, and as a result, the TBDs were decimated. All of Torpedo Squadron Eight's Devastators were shot down, and only a handful from VT-6 and VT-5 returned to their ships. None inflicted any real damage upon their targets. But while the torpedo planes had the undivided attention of the Japanese, the SBDs arrived overhead and began their dives on the four carriers. Bombs and torpedoes had been removed from their magazines and were exposed as the Japanese rearmed their aircraft. Therefore, the attack by the Dauntlesses could not have been better timed if it had been planned that way. In four minutes, three of the four carriers had been turned into sinking burning hulks. With them went dozens of aircraft, and more importantly, the Imperial Japanese Navy's best pilots were killed. Only HIRYU escaped destruction, and she too was sunk the following day. But before Dauntlesses disposed of the fourth Japanese carrier, her aircraft severely damaged YORKTOWN. Submarine I-168 then added a few torpedo hits that finished the carrier.

Again, the Americans had lost one carrier, but the Japanese lost four of their finest fleet carriers. It was a blow from which they would never recover, and it turned the tide of the war in the Pacific. The Midway invasion force had to retire, and the atoll remained safely in American hands.

All four Japanese carriers sunk at Midway were destroyed by Dauntless dive bombers. Although the submarine NAUTILUS fired torpedoes at one of the carriers, post-war evidence indicated that the torpedoes failed to detonate, and one of them was found floating by Japanese crewmen who clung to it until they were rescued. But although the fatal blows were delivered by SBDs, it should not be thought that they alone won the battle. Every Devastator crew who died trying to score a hit with an unreliable torpedo, and every Wildcat pilot who helped protect the bombers also contributed immeasurably to the ultimate outcome---as did a famous elusive lady known as LUCK.

While the Dauntless is best known for its actions at the battles of Coral Sea and Midway, its contributions elsewhere were also significantly important. In the fierce fighting for Guadalcanal, Marine SBDs of the Cactus Air Force on Henderson Field flew vital missions including many against the "Tokyo Express" as it attempted to reinforce and resupply the Japanese on the besieged island. Navy Dauntlesses, operating from the WASP (CV-7), ENTERPRISE (CV-6) and SARATOGA (CV-3), also participated in the Battle of the Eastern Solomons of which the fighting for Guadalcanal was a part. SBDs from the SARATOGA sank the carrier RYUJO on 24 August, but the Japanese submarine I-19 sank the WASP on 15 September.

While the battle for Guadalcanal and the Eastern Solomons raged on one side of the world, the North African campaign, known as Operation Torch, was under-

![Hangar bay photo]

Because Dauntlesses did not have folding wings, they were often suspended by cables from the overhead in the hangar bays of carriers. SBD-5s can be seen here aboard the USS YORKTOWN, (CV-10). (National Archives)

Details of the hoist cable are shown here. This cable remained in the aircraft at all times. (U. S. Navy)

9

An SBD-4 taxis forward to its take-off position aboard the USS RANGER (CV-4) during Operation Torch. The fact that this is an SBD-4 can be ascertained from the carburetor scoop on the cowling and the rounded hub of the Hamilton Standard propeller. The combination of these two features could be found only on the SBD-4.
(U. S. Navy via Ethell)

way in the Atlantic and the Mediterranean Sea. The carrier RANGER (CV-4) and the escort carriers SANGAMON (CVE-26), SUWANEE (CVE-27), and SANTEE (CVE-29) were all involved in Torch. All of these ships, except SUWANEE, had Dauntlesses in their air groups, and most of these were SBD-4s.

A year later, in October 1943, RANGER participated in Operation Leader, a raid against Axis shipping in Scandinavian waters, where her Dauntlesses saw limited combat.

Otherwise, the SBD's role in the Atlantic was of little consequence. Of the numerous escort carriers that hunted U-boats beginning in 1943, only SANTEE operated any Dauntlesses. Land-based SBDs patrolled the Caribbean, but saw little action.

In the Pacific it was quite a different story. By early 1943, the victories at Midway and Guadalcanal had helped turn the tide in the Pacific, but there were many hard-fought battles ahead. American strength was growing every day, while the Japanese were increasingly on the defensive. New ESSEX class carriers began joining the fleet, and more aircraft were needed for them.

By this time, the Navy had hoped that the Dauntless would be replaced by the larger SB2C Helldiver, but problems had plagued the development of the Helldiver and delayed its introduction into service. So as the Wild-

cats were replaced with Hellcats, and the Devastators were replaced with Avengers, the Dauntless still remained the primary dive bomber in use aboard carriers and land bases throughout the Pacific in 1943. In fact, the first operational use of the Helldiver did not occur until November 1943 when VB-17 flew missions against Rabaul.

As the Dauntless remained in service, it was continually improved. SBD-4s first arrived in operational units during the closing months of 1942, and some saw action during the North African campaign. This version of the Dauntless was similar to the SBD-3, but it had a 24-volt electrical system and a Hamilton Standard Hydromatic propeller with a smooth rounded hub. SBD-5s began replacing earlier versions in early 1943, and this variant had the R-1820-60 which provided a much needed additional 200 horsepower than that available on any of the previous models. The -60 engine did not require the carburetor scoop on top of the cowling, and this became an identifying feature of the SBD-5 and subsequent SBD-6. Another welcome improvement was the reflector gunsight which replaced the three-power telescope. To increase range, external fuel tanks could be carried under the wings. The SBD-6 had a further increase in power with the installation of the R-1820-66 engine which produced 1,350 horsepower. Otherwise, it was identical

The last of the line was the SBD-6. Unlike most other combat aircraft of World War II, every variant of the Dauntless was put into production and operational service. This was due in part because the changes made to the design from one version to the next were rather simple and few in number.
(National Archives)

Fairchild aerial cameras were sometimes carried in the aft cockpit of SBDs to take reconnaissance photographs and to show the results of combat strikes. (National Archives)

to the SBD-5. Very few SBD-6s ever made it to combat units. Instead, most served as trainers in the United States.

Even after enough of the bugs were eliminated from the Helldiver to permit its use aboard carriers, the Dauntless continued to be used in considerable numbers into the first few months of 1944. They participated in their last carrier battle during strikes against Ozawa's carriers in June 1944. In that action, only one of twenty-seven SBDs was lost to enemy action, and another three were lost operationally. By comparison, fifty SB2C Helldivers participated in the same strike, and only five returned to their carriers. More than half of the Helldivers ditched into the sea as they ran out of fuel, while the rest were lost due to damage sustained in combat. It is no wonder that SBD pilots openly stated a preference for the Dauntless over its replacement. But in July 1944, the Dauntlesses flew their last missions from carriers during an attack on Guam. VB-10 aboard ENTERPRISE was the unit that flew the last carrier-based SBD mission in the Pacific.

Although the Navy had changed over to the Helldiver, the Marines continued to make good use of the Dauntless from land bases. From Luzon and later from Mindanao, SBDs from Marine Air Groups Twenty-four and Thirty-two supported McArthur's forces in the Philippines.

The German's successful use of the Ju-87 Stuka prompted a small interest in dive bombing within the U. S. Army Air Force. General George Marshall insisted that dive bombing be a part of the doctrine and training of the USAAF, and this prompted the order of seventy-eight SBD-3s built to Army specifications. Designated the A-24 Banshee, these aircraft did not have the arresting hook used for carrier landings, and they were equipped with the large pneumatic tail wheel used on land-based Dauntlesses by the Marines. The subsequent A-24A and A-24B were the Army equivalents of the SBD-4 and SBD-5 respectively.

The Army had intended to use the Banshee primarily as a dive bombing trainer while it awaited deliveries of the Army's version of the Helldiver designated the A-25. But the delays with the Helldiver program did result in a few A-24s seeing combat. Those that did see action with the 91st Bombardment Squadron and the 8th Bombardment Group achieved very little in the way of success. This was due more to the Army's lack of experience with dive bombing and its doctrinal preference for larger strategic bombers than it was due to any problems with the aircraft itself. In fact, the USAAF never mastered the art of dive bombing with the A-24 or the A-25, nor did it ever put this method of bombing into any widespread use.

Four countries other than the United States also operated SBDs and A-24s during World War II. New Zealand flew eighteen SBD-3s, twenty-seven SBD-4s, and twenty-three SBD-5s in the Pacific, while the Free French flew both SBD-5s and A-24Bs in Europe. French Dauntlesses were flown against the communists in Indo-China during 1949, thus becoming the last of the type to serve in combat. Great Britain received nine SBD-5s which it designated the Dauntless Mark I. These aircraft were used for evaluation purposes, but no further Dauntlesses were obtained by the British. Mexico received several A-24Bs which were used for patrol missions in the Caribbean during World War II. After the war, these Banshees served as border patrol aircraft until 1959, thus being the last SBD/A-24s to be used by any national government.

Throughout the war, the Dauntless had the lowest loss rate for any American carrier aircraft. In his book The Dauntless Dive Bomber of World War II, Barrett Tillman reports that SBDs shot down 138 Japanese aircraft, while less than eighty Dauntless were lost to enemy aircraft. It sank over 300,000 tons of enemy shipping, and included in this figure were six Japanese aircraft carriers. Scores of other ships were damaged by SBDs. Hundreds of shore-based targets were destroyed, and the Army and Marines received plenty of close air support from the Dauntless. When all of the records and achievements are totaled for the various aircraft that saw action in the Pacific during World War II, it is difficult to find any with more timely and significant contributions than those of the **S**low **B**ut **D**eadly Dauntless.

DAUNTLESS VARIANTS
SBD-1

The SBD-1 was not really a combat-ready aircraft, but it could be characterized as having the greatest eye appeal when painted in its pre-war colors. Note the natural metal propeller. **(National Archives)**

The initial order for Dauntlesses included fifty-seven SBD-1s, all of which were delivered to the Marine Corps. The first -1s were accepted by the Marines in June 1940, and were assigned to VMB-2 of Marine Air Group Eleven at Quantico, Virginia. More Dauntlesses were soon sent to VMB-1 of Marine Air Group Twenty-One at Ewa, Hawaii. These two squadrons were redesignated VMSB-232 and VMSB-132, respectively, by the end of 1941.

The physical feature which identified the SBD-1 was its larger carburetor air scoop on top of the cowling. Otherwise, its external appearance was like the SBD-2 that followed. The -1 was also the only Dauntless variant to be painted in any of the colorful pre-war schemes.

Another reference has reported that the SBD-1 had two forward-firing .30-caliber machine guns in the cowling, but official manuals reveal that these were in fact .50 caliber guns as on all variants of the SBD. It has also been reported that the larger pneumatic tail wheel, intended for land-based operations, was designed for the Army's A-24 Banshee. However, these larger tail wheels were actually developed for Marine Dauntlesses, and even early SBD-1s were soon fitted with the larger pneumatic tail wheel.

As a combat aircraft, the SBD-1 lacked many of the essentials. It did not have self-sealing tanks or armor

Details of the propeller and cowling on an SBD-1 are visible in this photograph. Note the three cowl flaps and the details of the ventilation slot further aft on the fuselage. The large carburetor scoop is visible on top of the cowling. The features of the SBD-2 were identical except that the carburetor scoop was not quite as large.
(National Archives)

protection for its crew. It carried only 210 gallons of fuel distributed in four tanks, all of which were located in the center wing section. Two of the tanks had a capacity of ninety gallons each, while two small auxiliary tanks held fifteen gallons each. This gave the -1 a maximum bombing range of only 860 miles and a scouting range of 1,165 miles.

All SBD-1s stationed in Hawaii were destroyed or damaged during the Japanese attack on Pearl Harbor, but by then the combat-ready SBD-3s were rolling off the production lines to replace the SBD-1s and SBD-2s.

Eight SBD-1s were fitted with cameras and redesignated SBD-1Ps.

SBD-1 Bureau Numbers were as follows:
　　1596 through 1631
　　1735 through 1755

SBD-1 DATA

Empty Weight	5,903 pounds
Maximum Weight	9,790 pounds
Maximum Speed	253 miles per hour
Cruising Speed	142 miles per hour
Rate of Climb	1,730 feet per minute
Service Ceiling	29,600 feet
Bombing Range	860 miles
Scouting Range	1,165 miles

These SBD-1s are painted in the overall gray scheme used during most of 1941. These land-based aircraft belong to VMSB-132, which was the same Marine squadron that had formerly been designated VMB-1. This photograph provides evidence that the larger pneumatic tail wheel was developed for Marine land-based Dauntlesses rather than for the A-24 Banshee as reported elsewhere. This photo was taken in 1941, before any A-24s were ordered.

(USMC via Ethell)

Major details of the pilot's cockpit in an SBD-1 can be seen here. This cockpit differed very little from that in the SBD-3 shown on pages 36 and 37. Note the round counters for the two forward machine guns which are located on either side of the main instrument panel.

(National Archives)

Early Dauntlesses had flotation equipment mounted on both sides of the forward fuselage. These bags were released if the aircraft was ditched in the water in order to keep it afloat. This equipment was standard on the SBD-1 and the SBD-2, but it was deleted beginning with the SBD-3 as a weight-saving measure. *(National Archives)*

SBD-2

Although the SBD-2 had improvements over the SBD-1, it still was not entirely ready for combat. This was the first variant to be assigned to Navy units, and a few saw combat action during the first half of 1942 before being replaced by SBD-3s. The SBD-2 introduced the smaller carburetor air scoop on top of the cowling that was carried forward to the SBD-3 and SBD-4 as well. **(National Archives)**

Along with the fifty-seven SBD-1s, the initial order of Dauntlesses also included eighty-seven SBD-2s for the Navy. These aircraft began to enter service in November 1940 aboard the ENTERPRISE (CV-6) and LEXINGTON (CV-2).

The noticeable external difference between the SBD-1 and the SBD-2 was that the carburetor air scoop on the cowling was reduced in size. Otherwise, the two versions looked the same. But inside, there was an important difference. The two fifteen-gallon fuel tanks were eliminated, and two larger sixty-five-gallon tanks were placed in the outer wing sections. This raised the total amount of fuel to 310 gallons which provided a bombing range of 1,225 miles and a scouting range of almost 1,400 miles.

An SBD-2 from the ENTERPRISE was the first Dauntless to sink an enemy ship when Lieutenant Clarence Dickinson sank the Japanese submarine I-70 on 10 December, 1941. This was particularly sweet revenge for LT Dickinson, because he had been shot down in another SBD-2 over Pearl Harbor only three days earlier. But Dickinson's gunner had destroyed an attacking Japanese aircraft before the Dauntless was mortally wounded. LT Dickinson bailed out to safety, but his gunner was killed.

Although a few SBD-2s did continue to serve in combat through the Battle of Midway in June 1942, most of them had been replaced with the SBD-3 during the early months of that year.

Fourteen SBD-2s were converted for the photographic reconnaissance mission, and these were given the designation SBD-2P.

SBD-2 Bureau Numbers were as follows:
 2102 through 2188

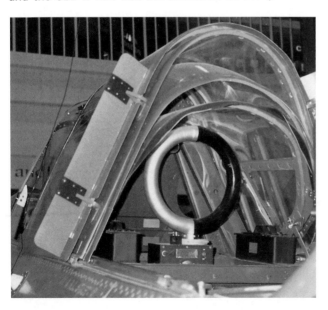

Some early Dauntlesses had loop antennas located between the two cockpits as seen here, however it would be incorrect to say that this antenna was a standard feature. Photographic evidence indicates that these loop antennas were used on fewer and fewer aircraft as time went on. Radios and other electronic gear not only varied considerably from variant to variant but also from aircraft to aircraft.

SBD-2 DATA

Empty Weight	6,293 pounds
Maximum Weight	10,360 pounds
Maximum Speed	252 miles per hour
Cruising Speed	148 miles per hour
Rate of Climb	1,080 feet per minute
Service Ceiling	26,000 feet
Bombing Range	1,225 miles
Scouting Range	1,370 miles

SBD-3

The SBD-3 may not have been the definitive variant of the Dauntless, but it was the one which did the most damage to the Imperial Japanese Navy when it really counted during the desperate days of 1942. This SBD-3 is painted in the overall gray scheme used during 1941. Note the lack of a fuselage insignia. The stencilling on the door of the life raft container reads "LIFE RAFT & EMERGENCY RATIONS." *(National Archives)*

For the most part, it was the SBD-3 that gained the glory and achieved the most spectacular successes at Coral Sea, Midway, and the Eastern Solomons during 1942. A total of 584 -3s were delivered to the Navy and Marines, and these had better armor protection and self-sealing fuel tanks. Early production SBD-3s had the single .30-caliber flexible gun in the rear cockpit, but later examples had twin guns and a large single ammunition box as well. This not only doubled the amount of firepower for the rear cockpit, it also eliminated the need to change ammunition boxes in the heat of combat. The twin flexible gun mount and the large ammunition box was also retrofitted in the field to earlier -3s beginning in mid-1942,

and these were in place in most, if not all, SBD-3s that fought in the Battle of Midway. With its increased firepower and nimble handling qualities, the SBD-3 and subsequent variants held their own against Japanese aircraft. They were even used as inner combat air patrol aircraft, a job usually assigned to fighters, and they scored impressive results against enemy aircraft that were attacking American ships.

Externally, the SBD-3 differed from the previous -2 only in having a slightly larger ventilation slot on the cowling. Although the SBD-3s were originally fitted with a spinner on the propeller hub, these were often removed, thus revealing a cylindrical hub with a flat forward end.

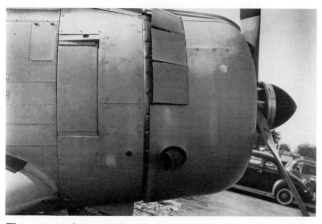 

These two photographs illustrate the details on the cowling of an SBD -3. In the photo at left, the three cowl flaps are open, while the view at right shows them closed. Compare the differences in the ventilation slot with that used on the SBD-1 and SBD-2 as illustrated on page 12. Also note that the carburetor intake on top of the cowling is much smaller in the vertical dimension than on the SBD-1. This same cowling and ventilation slot was used on the SBD-4, however, the type of propeller was changed. *(National Archives)*

An SBD-3 is shown on the elevator aboard the USS SANTEE (CVE-29). One shortcoming of the Dauntless was that it did not have folding wings, and this proved to be a problem on aircraft carriers. Note how this SBD has to be positioned on the elevator at a slight diagonal angle in order for it to clear the edges. There is very little room to spare at the wing tips and at the nose and tail of the aircraft. The angle of this photograph provides a good look at the features of the aircraft and the weathering on the upper surfaces. Note that the aircraft does not have the yellow surround on the fuselage insignia, meaning that this photograph was taken before or after Operation Torch. SANTEE was one of the carriers that participated in the North African campaign. *(National Archives)*

The R-1820-52 engine replaced the -32 used in the SBD-1 and -2, however, it provided the same 1,000 horsepower as the earlier versions of the engine.

Forty-three SBD-3s received the SBD-3P designation after being converted to perform the photo-reconnaissance mission.

SBD-3 Bureau Numbers were as follows:
    4518 through 4691
    03185 through 03384
    06492 through 06701

SBD-3 DATA

Empty Weight	6,345 pounds
Maximum Weight	10,400 pounds
Maximum Speed	250 miles per hour
Cruising Speed	152 miles per hour
Rate of Climb	1,190 feet per minute
Service Ceiling	27,100 feet
Bombing Range	1,345 miles
Scouting Range	1,580 miles

A telescopic sight was used on all Dauntless variants from the SBD-1 through the SBD-4. These two photographs show the sight in SBD-3, 06508.

SBD-4

With the yellow surround of Operation Torch added to their fuselage insignias, these SBD-4s fly over the new escort carrier SANGAMON (CVE-26) during the North African campaign. Some sources report that SBD-3s were the only Dauntlesses used during this action, but most photographs show the Hamilton Standard propeller with its rounded hub that was first used on the SBD-4. This is not to say that SBD-3s did not participate in Operation Torch, but clearly, many photographs taken aboard RANGER (CV-4) and SANGAMON are of SBD-4s. Of particular interest in this photograph is the non-standard wire antenna leading down to the top of the left wing of the aircraft from which this photograph was taken. (National Archives)

The SBD-4 was introduced into operational service in late 1942, and some saw duty during Operation Torch. With the addition of more electronic gear inside the aircraft, the electrical system was upgraded to a 24-volt system from the previous 12-volt system. Both the primary and emergency fuel pumps were electrically powered. Externally, the SBD-4 differed from the -3 only by having a Hamilton Standard Hydromatic propeller. This propeller had a wider chord and more rounded tips than that used on earlier Dauntlesses. It also had a smaller hub which was rounded on the front end. This was the propeller that would also be used on future SBD-5 and -6 variants. Although the SBD-4 was the first Dauntless that could be equipped with radar, the YAGI antennas under the wings did not come into widespread use until the subsequent SBD-5.

A total of 780 SBD-4s were produced, and most of these were delivered to the U. S. Marines. However, this variant did serve in several Navy carrier-based squadrons, most notably those aboard the RANGER (CV-4), INDEPENDENCE (CVL-22), and SANGAMON (CVE-26).

SBD-4 Bureau Numbers were as follows:
06702 through 06991
10371 through 10806

SBD-4 DATA

Empty Weight . . . . 6,360 pounds
Maximum Weight . . . . 10,480 pounds
Maximum Speed . . . . 245 miles per hour
Cruising Speed . . . . 150 miles per hour
Rate of Climb . . . . 1,150 feet per minute
Service Ceiling . . . . 26,700 feet
Bombing Range . . . . 1,300 miles
Scouting Range . . . . 1,450 miles

An SBD-4 recovers back aboard the USS RANGER (CV-4) during Operation Torch. Again, the fact that this is an SBD-4 can be determined because the rounded hub of the Hamilton Standard Hydromatic propeller and the carburetor intake are both visible. Both of these features together could only be found on an SBD-4.

(U. S. Navy via Ethell)

SBD-5

This view from above clearly illustrates the fact that the carburetor scoop was removed completely from the SBD-5. Note the small wire whip antenna just to the right of the clear position light on the spine of the aft fuselage. The number and location of whip antennas varied considerably depending on the electronic equipment carried in the aircraft. These aircraft clearly have the red surround on their national insignias, and this dates the photograph in the late 1943 time period. However, there are no markings that indicate to which unit or carrier these Dauntlesses were assigned.

A total of 2,965 SBD-5s were produced, far exceeding the number of any other Dauntless variant. The first of these was delivered during May 1943, and -5s quickly began replacing the older versions. The SBD-5 (and subsequent SBD-6) could be identified visually by the lack of a carburetor air scoop that had appeared on all previous variants. The ventilation slot on each side of the forward fuselage was larger in vertical dimension, and it was situated further aft than on earlier SBDs. Additionally,

there was only one flap on each side of the cowling instead of the three used on earlier variants.

More important to the pilot was the fact that the old three-power telescopic sight was replaced with a reflector gunsight. Horsepower increased to 1,200 with the installation of the R-1820-60 engine, and range could be extended through the use of two external fuel tanks. Although the SBD-4 had the capability to carry and employ airborne radar sets, these began to appear in con-

The SBD-5 had only one cowl flap on each side as opposed to three on earlier variants. The ventilation slot on the side of the forward fuselage was longer in the vertical dimension and further aft than before. This slot can be seen directly below the radio antenna mast in both of these photographs.

The SBD-5 was produced in greater numbers than any other Dauntless variant. This -5 is shown undergoing maintenance on Majuro. Dauntlesses that operated from land bases usually had treaded tires on their main gear and the larger pneumatic tail wheel. This particular SBD-5 has both of these features. Note the YAGI radar antenna under the wing and the fact that the retractable landing light has been covered over with a solid metal panel.

(National Archives)

siderable numbers on SBD-5s. Aircraft equipped with the radar could be identified by the two movable YAGI antennas, one of which was located under each wing. The scope for the radar was placed in the rear cockpit under the fixed center section of the canopy.

SBD-5 Bureau Numbers were as follows:
    10807 through 11066
    28059 through 29213
    35922 through 36421
    36433 through 36932
    54050 through 54599

SBD-5A Bureau Numbers were as follows:
    09693 through 09752

SBD-5 DATA

Empty Weight	6,533 pounds
Maximum Weight	10,700 pounds
Maximum Speed	252 miles per hour
Cruising Speed	139 miles per hour
Rate of Climb	1,700 feet per minute
Service Ceiling	24,300 feet
Bombing Range	1,115 miles
Scouting Range	1,565 miles

A reflector sight replaced the primitive telescopic sight on the SBD-5 and the subsequent SBD-6.

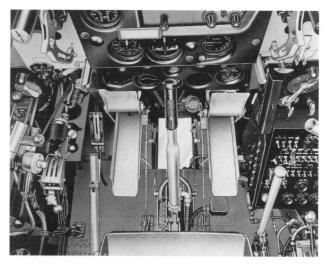

The floor of the pilot's cockpit is shown here. As with all versions of the Dauntless, the SBD-5 had a hole in the floor to allow the pilot to see out the window in the lower fuselage. The electrical distribution panel can be seen at the far right. Colors in the SBD-5 cockpits were similar to those illustrated for the SBD-3 on pages 36 through 39. *(National Archives)*

This is the main instrument panel in an SBD-5. The primary differences from the previous variants include the reflector gunsight and the autopilot controls on the upper panel. Note that the two fixed guns are not present in this photograph. *(National Archives)*

Here is a look at the left side of the pilot's cockpit. Note the map case located high on the wall. Otherwise, the features are very similar to those shown for the SBD-3 on pages 36 and 37. *(National Archives)*

A canteen was mounted on the aft bulkhead of the pilot's cockpit on the left side. The seat has been removed from this SBD-5 during restoration.

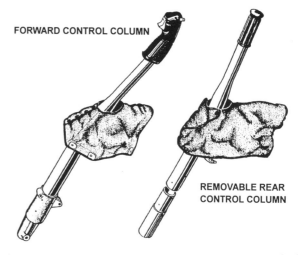

FORWARD CONTROL COLUMN

REMOVABLE REAR CONTROL COLUMN

This drawing shows the control columns used in both the front and rear cockpits of the Dauntless.

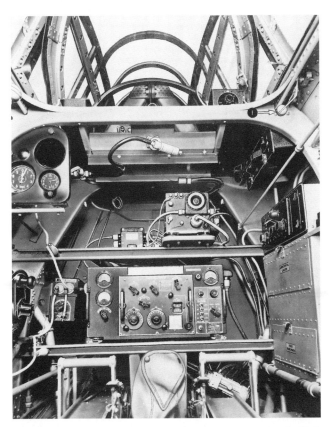

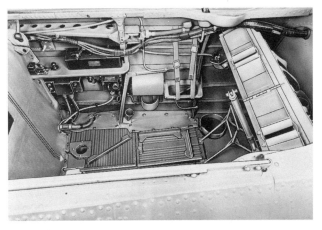

This is the right side of the aft cockpit with the guns and turret removed. The oxygen system is not in place, but would be mounted to the right and held in place by the two straps that can be seen just forward of the ammunition box. Note that the snap-in protective cover for the forward end of the cockpit is in place and can be seen to the left in this photograph. (National Archives)

With the snap-in protective cover removed, the basic flight instruments and the electronic gear at the forward end of the rear cockpit of an SBD-5 can be seen here. The confidential storage lockers are visible at right.
(National Archives)

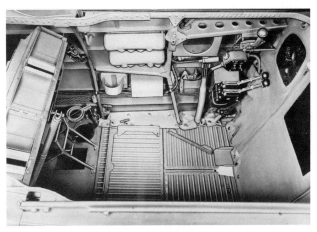

The left side of the rear cockpit is shown in this view. The clear panels of flexible plastic in the snap-in cover can be seen, and they allow the gunner/radio operator to view the instruments and radio gear even with the cover in place. The canvas containers for the flares are visible in the center of the photo, but the pistol is not in its place. Note that the aft control column is stowed in its place against the side of the cockpit. (National Archives)

A canteen was also located in the aft cockpit, and it was attached to the aft bulkhead on the left side. This photograph was taken in an SBD-5 during restoration.

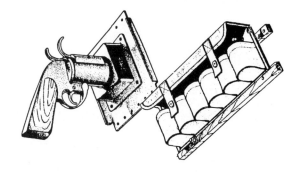

This drawing shows the flare pistol in position to be fired through the port in the left side of the aft cockpit.

SBD-6

The SBD-6 had only minor improvements over the SBD-5. By the time this variant was in full production, the Curtiss SB2C Helldiver was replacing the Dauntless in many squadrons. As a result, a considerable number of SBD-6s were used in training units. **(National Archives)**

The final variant of the Dauntless was the SBD-6, and it differed from the SBD-5 only in that it was powered by the R-1820-66 engine which produced 1,350 horsepower. One SBD-5, BuNo. 28830, was originally fitted with this engine and served as the XSBD-6 prototype. The engine change resulted in no externally recognizable physical differences between the -5 and -6.

By the time the SBD-6 went into production, the SB2C Helldiver was finally ready for operational service and was replacing the Dauntless aboard U. S. carriers. As a result, the production run for the SBD-6 was only 450 aircraft, and many of these did not make it to the combat areas. Instead, most of them were relegated to training duties within the United States.

Bureau Numbers for the SBD-6 included the following:
54600 through 55049.

SBD-6 DATA

Empty Weight	6,554 pounds
Maximum Weight	10,882 pounds
Maximum Speed	262 miles per hour
Cruising Speed	143 miles per hour
Rate of Climb	1,710 feet per minute
Service Ceiling	28,600 feet
Bombing Range	1,230 miles
Scouting Range	1,700 miles

The SBD-5 and SBD-6 could carry external fuel tanks to increase range and patrolling time. Crewmen are shown here attaching a fuel tank to the wing rack of an SBD-6. (National Archives)

A-24 BANSHEE

Three versions of the Dauntless were modified for use in limited numbers by the U. S. Army Air Force. The aircraft was called the A-24 Banshee by the Army, and primarily because the leadership in the USAAF did not widely support the concept of dive bombing, the A-24 was not used extensively in combat. The few units that did see action achieved very little in the way of operational results. Note that the arresting hook has been removed, but that its attach point remains. A-24s had the larger pneumatic tail wheel intended for land operations. The standard paint scheme used on Banshees included olive drab upper and vertical surfaces and neutral gray undersides. The tail numbers are yellow. This aircraft is carrying a practice bomb dispenser under its left wing. (National Archives)

General George Marshall wanted to add dive bombers to the arsenal of the Army Air Force, and as a result, seventy-eight A-24 Banshees were ordered. These were similar to the SBD-3, but the arresting hook was removed. However, the actuator or hinge point for the hook was retained. Banshees were also fitted with the larger pneumatic tail wheel used on land-based Dauntlesses. Additionally, the A-24s did not have the two flare launchers in the aft fuselage, and therefore the two small doors on the lower left fuselage were not present. In addition to the A-24, ninety SBD-3s were also delivered to the USAAF and were produced under the designation SBD-3A. These also had the equipment associated with carrier operations deleted.

A-24As were similar to the SBD-4, and 170 were delivered to the USAAF. The 615 A-24Bs were comparable to the SBD-5, and additionally there were sixty SBD-5As delivered to the Army but subsequently turned over to the Marines.

Serial numbers were as follows:

A-24	41-15748 through 41-15823
A-24A	42-6772 through 42-6831
	42-60772 through 42-60881
A-24B	42-54285 through 42-54899

This Banshee was used for special testing at Wright Field. The large fairing under the fuselage appears to be a camera, but what the probes under the wings and the extra fairings on the cowling were for has not been determined. ((National Archives)

DIMENSIONS & SCALE DRAWINGS
DETAIL & SCALE 1/72nd SCALE FIVE-VIEW DRAWINGS

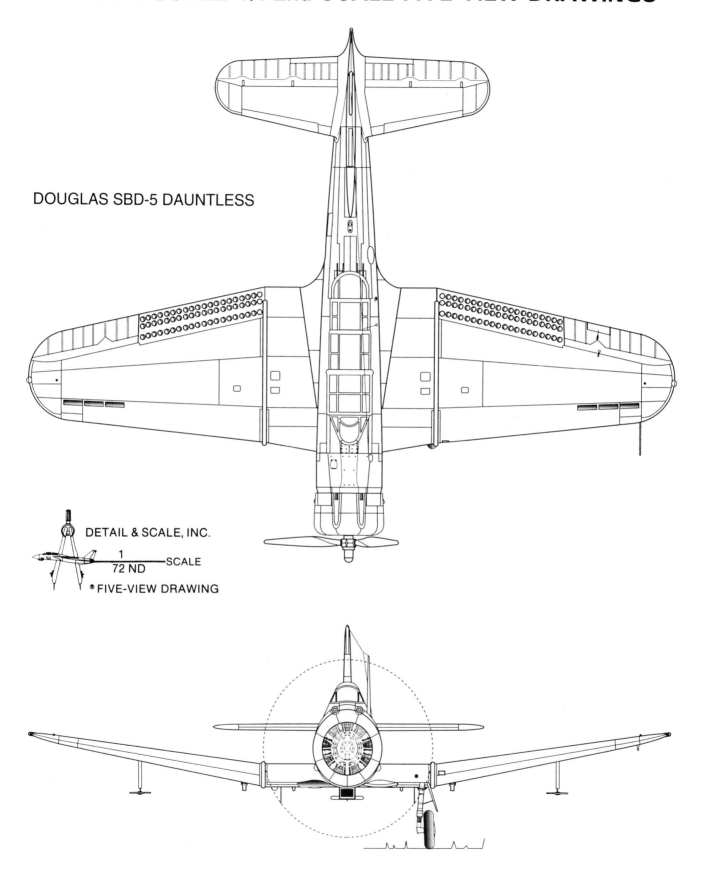

DOUGLAS SBD-5 DAUNTLESS

DETAIL & SCALE, INC.

$$\frac{1}{72 \text{ ND}}$$ SCALE

® FIVE-VIEW DRAWING

DETAIL & SCALE COPYRIGHT DRAWINGS BY LLOYD S. JONES

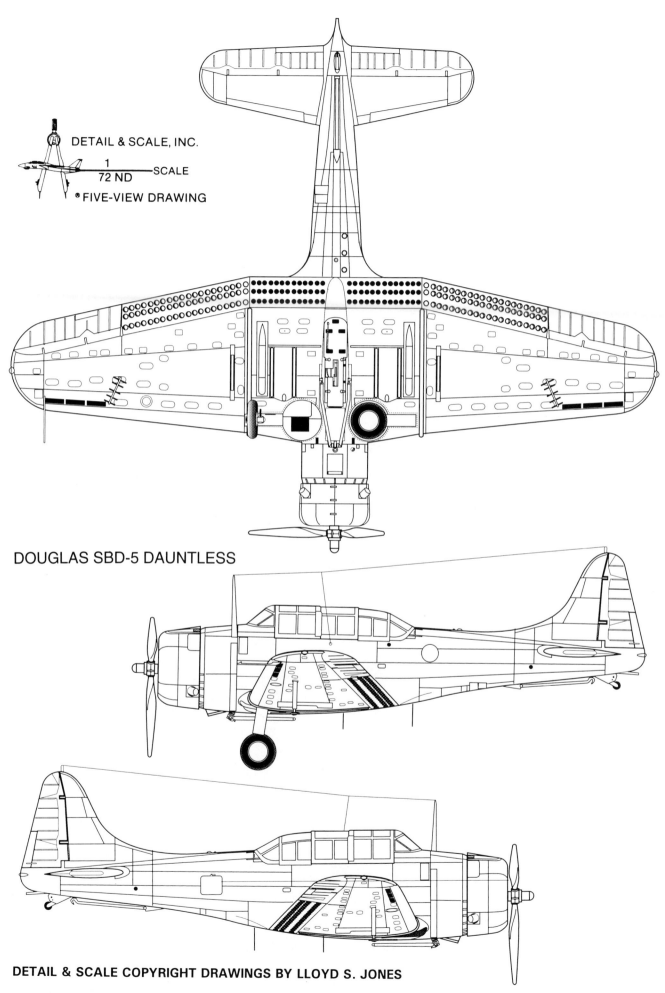

DETAIL & SCALE, INC.

$$\frac{1}{72\text{ ND}}$$ SCALE

® FIVE-VIEW DRAWING

DOUGLAS SBD-5 DAUNTLESS

DETAIL & SCALE COPYRIGHT DRAWINGS BY LLOYD S. JONES

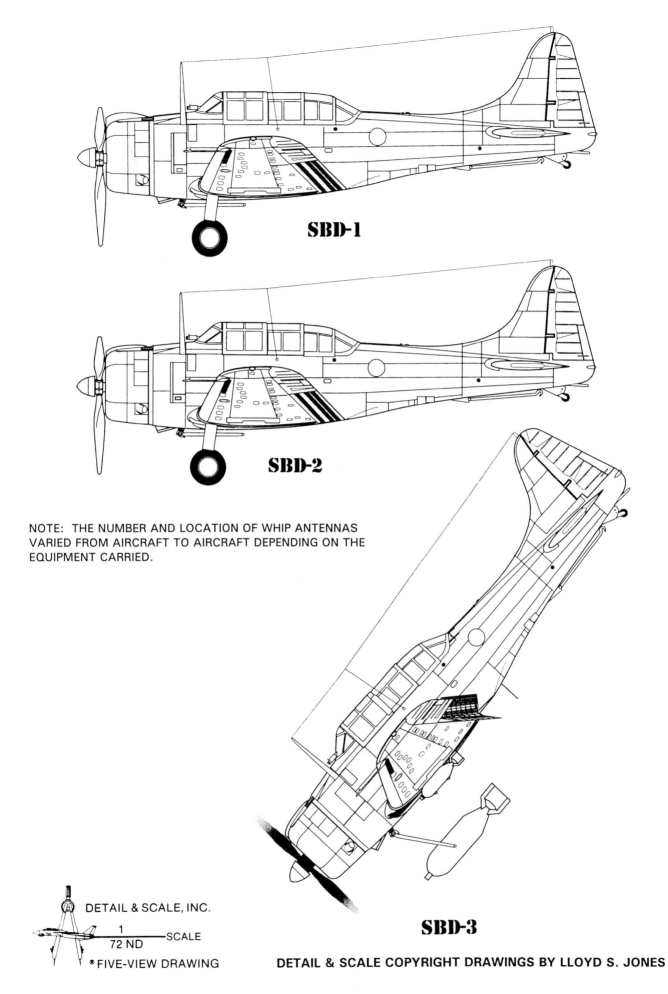

SBD-1

SBD-2

NOTE: THE NUMBER AND LOCATION OF WHIP ANTENNAS VARIED FROM AIRCRAFT TO AIRCRAFT DEPENDING ON THE EQUIPMENT CARRIED.

SBD-3

DETAIL & SCALE, INC.

1
——SCALE
72 ND

® FIVE-VIEW DRAWING

DETAIL & SCALE COPYRIGHT DRAWINGS BY LLOYD S. JONES

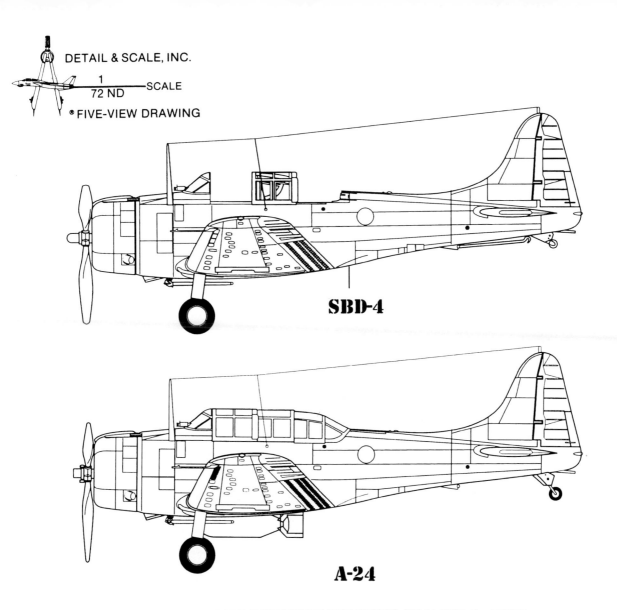

SBD-4

A-24

DETAIL & SCALE COPYRIGHT DRAWINGS BY LLOYD S. JONES

DAUNTLESS DIMENSIONS

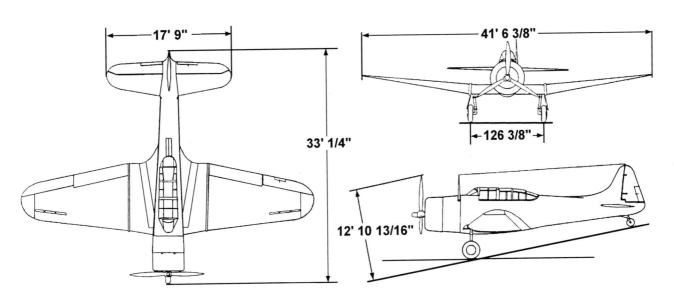

17' 9"

41' 6 3/8"

126 3/8"

33' 1/4"

12' 10 13/16"

DAUNTLESS DETAILS
CANOPY DETAILS

The canopy enclosure for all Dauntless variants consisted of five pieces, of which two were fixed and three were movable. There were no changes made to the canopy throughout the entire SBD series except that the windscreen was modified to delete the hole for the telescopic sight when the reflector sight was introduced on the SBD-5. These two photographs show the entire canopy structure from above. At left, the pilot's sliding canopy is partly open, while the gunner's canopy is closed. In the photograph at right, all sliding parts of the canopy are fully open. These photographs also reveal the two flat black, non-skid walkways on the wing roots.

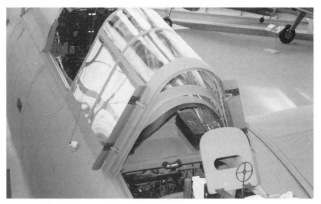

Left: In this view, the two sliding sections that cover the aft cockpit are stowed beneath the fixed center section. The pilot's sliding canopy is partly open. Note the actuators for the air flow deflectors on the aft framework of the fixed center section.

Above: With the pilot's sliding canopy all the way aft, the actuators move the spring-loaded air flow deflectors to the open position. The underside of the deflectors were chromate green, and the darker areas, where they contacted the actuators, were dark reddish brown.

A magnetic compass was attached to the top of the windscreen. The inside of the framework was painted chromate green.

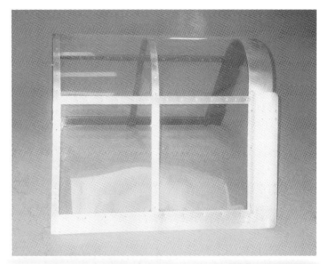

This is the pilot's sliding canopy with the spring-loaded air flow deflectors at the aft end (to the right in the photograph). This is the only part of the canopy with framework across the top in the center of the section.

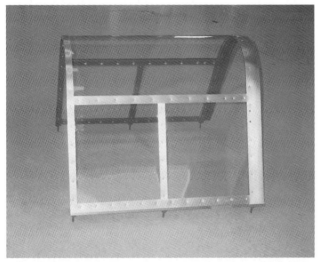

The fixed center section is shown here, however, the actuators for the air flow deflectors have not yet been installed. Note that the aft framework (to the right in the photograph) is wider than the forward framework.

Here is the sliding part that covered the aft cockpit. Again, the aft framework is wider than the forward framework. Note how the interior horizontal framework angles down as it gets further aft.

These two photographs show the aft-most sliding part of the canopy, and it is the section that covers the guns and ammunition box. Note the rubber weather strip around its rear framework. This section had a hinge that fit into the inside of the canopy rail on each side of the aircraft. The gunner tilted the section up to the position shown in these photographs, then slid it forward to its stowed position beneath the fixed center section.

LANDING GEAR DETAILS

The Dauntless had a simple but sturdy retractable main gear. There was only one door for each main gear, and it covered the strut when the gear was retracted. At left is the right main gear from the outside, while at right is a front view of the gear. Note the angle of the strut, wheel, and door with respect to the wing. The strut was not perpendicular to the wing, but the wheel was. Tires with no tread were the norm for earlier Dauntlesses, but treaded tires, originally intended primarily for land use, were seen more and more on later SBD variants even during carrier operations.

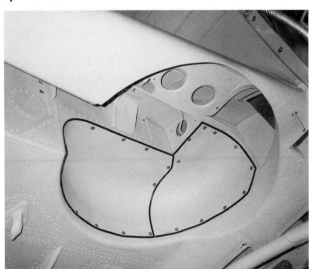

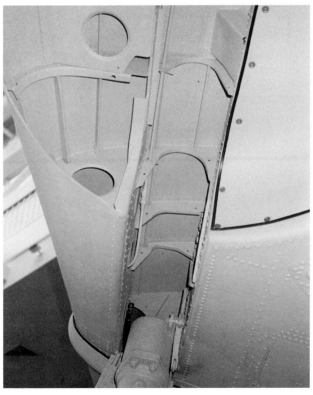

Above: This is a view of the inner portion of the right wheel well showing where the wheel and tire fit when the gear was retracted.

Right: The outer portion of the gear well is shown here. The strut fit into this area. The well was painted the same color as the undersides of the aircraft.

These two photographs show the left main gear from the inside and outside. The wheel was actually a spoked design, but it was almost always covered with a flat plate as shown here. The photograph at right reveals the details of the inside of the gear door. Of particular interest is the small brace between the strut and the door. Also note the brake line running from the wing down to the inside of the wheel.

Here is a look at the left main landing gear in the retracted position. The entire wheel is exposed, however the strut is covered by the door which is flush with the underside of the wing.

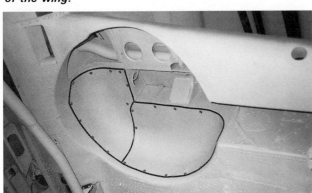 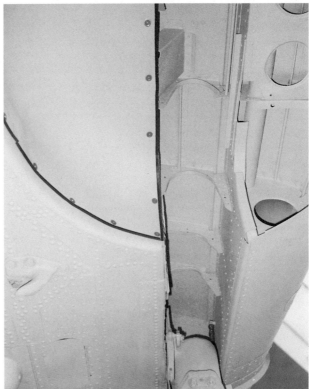

The interior of the left main gear well can be seen in these two photos. At left is the area for the wheel, while at right is a view which shows where the strut retracts.

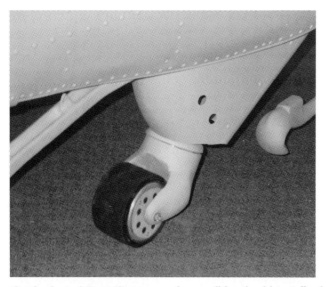

Carrier-based Dauntlesses used a small hard rubber tail wheel as illustrated in these two photographs. The tail wheel was not retractable.

Details of the tail wheel are better illustrated in this photo of the wheel before it was installed on the aircraft. The wheel is a natural metal that is a silver-gray in color.

On many land-based Navy and Marine Dauntlesses and on the A-24 Banshee, a larger pneumatic tail wheel was used. At left is the fully installed tail wheel and its fairing, but in the photograph at right, the tail cone has been removed to show the supporting structure for the wheel.

COLOR GALLERY

On 30 December, 1940, a directive was issued that ended the use of colorful paint schemes and markings in use on U. S. Navy and Marine aircraft prior to that time. Within a few weeks, the aircraft were being painted in an overall light gray scheme. The light gray paint was non-specular to reduce visibility, and the national insignia was carried on the top left and bottom right wing panels and on both sides of the fuselage. Using flat white paint, twelve-inch high numbers and letters were painted on the fuselage to denote the squadron number, mission, and individual aircraft number. In this photograph, SBD-2s from Scouting 5 can be seen flying in formation. Note the red antenna mast on the squadron commander's aircraft at the lower right.   (U. S. Navy photo via Ethell)

On 13 October, 1941, the overall gray paint scheme was replaced with a two tone scheme of non-specular blue-gray on the upper surfaces, and non-specular light gray on the lower surfaces of the aircraft. The numbers and letters on the sides of the fuselage were painted flat black beginning in December, shortly after the attack on Pearl Harbor. This photograph shows SBD-3s of VB-6 and VS-6 aboard the USS ENTERPRISE in early 1942. The aircraft in the background with the folded wings are TBD-1 Devastators of Torpedo Squadron Six (VT-6).
(U. S. Navy photo via Ethell)

On aircraft participating in Operation Torch, a yellow surround was added to the national insignias on the fuselage, but not to the insignias on the wings. Dauntlesses and Wildcats can be seen here on the deck of the USS SANGAMON (CVE-26) during the North African campaign. Note that the national insignia is in all four positions on the wings.
(U. S. Navy photo via Ethell)

SBD-5s, F6Fs, and TBFs can be seen on the aft flight deck of an unidentified carrier in late 1943. Note the large yellow numbers on the sides of the Dauntlesses. Although the SBDs are still in the blue-gray over light gray scheme, the Hellcats and Avengers are in the tri-color scheme authorized in February 1943. The national insignia was changed to have a white bar on each side of the star and disc on 29 June, 1943, and this style of insignia is visible on these aircraft. From 29 June to 17 September, 1943, the national insignia was to have a red surround, and the Dauntless at left appears to have this red surround as part of the insignia on its fuselage.
(U. S. Navy photo via Ethell)

Standard markings for the second half of 1942 can be seen here. Note the red "no step" stripe on the trailing edge of the wing just outboard of the walkway. The propeller tips were still painted in three colors, these being red, yellow, and blue beginning at the tip and working in. By the time this photograph was taken, squadron numbers and mission letters had been removed from the fuselage, leaving only the aircraft number in flat black.
(National Archives via Bell)

The tri-color paint scheme is shown to good effect on this SBD-6. It consisted of semi-gloss Sea Blue on the upper surfaces, Intermediate Blue on the vertical surfaces, and non-specular Insignia White on the undersides of the aircraft. Contrary to information published elsewhere, the official directive for this scheme did not have the Sea Blue extend down the sides of the fuselage to meet the Sea Blue color on the tops of the wings. Although this was often done in the field, it was not the authorized pattern for the Dauntless. (U. S. Navy photo via Ethell)

An example of the non-standard use of the tri-color scheme on a Dauntless is shown here as this SBD-5 lands aboard a carrier. Note that the darker color, which is semi-gloss Sea Blue, is painted down the sides of the fuselage to meet with the same color on the top of the wings. Although it was rather common to see aircraft painted this way, it did not reflect the officially authorized pattern for this scheme. When the tri-color scheme was authorized, the red, yellow, and blue stripes on the propeller tips were replaced with a single five inch yellow band on each tip.
(National Archives)

The pattern for the tri-color scheme can be seen on this SBD-5 as it taxis to its take-off position for a raid on Rabaul in May 1944. Unofficial colors were often used, and this is apparent here. Although it is difficult to tell what the darker color is, the middle color is certainly not Intermediate Blue, but is more of a gray instead. A significant amount of modification was allowed for commanders at ground bases, however, the colors used on carrier based aircraft were usually very close to the standards set forth in the official directives. *(U. S. Navy photo via Ethell)*

A two-color scheme was adopted for aircraft operating in the Atlantic during 1944. It consisted of Dark Gull Gray on the upper surfaces, and Insignia White on the vertical surfaces and undersides of the aircraft. For this scheme, the Dark Gull Gray was extended down the side of the fuselage to join with the same color on the tops of the wings. These are SBD-5s on patrol in the Caribbean area.

(U. S. Navy photo via Ethell)

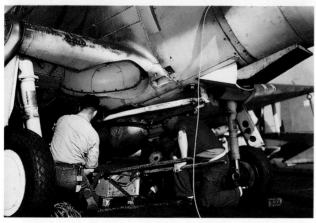

At left is a photograph of crewmen loading a bomb on an SBD-5. The aircraft is painted in the tri-color scheme. Note the fake gun ports painted on the leading edge of the left wing. At right, mechanics work on the engine of another SBD-5. Note the aircraft's number painted on the lower lip of the cowling. *(U. S. Navy photos via Ethell)*

SBD-3 PILOT'S COCKPIT DETAILS & COLORS

The area under the windscreen of an SBD-3 is shown here without the windscreen or telescopic sight in place. The forward part of this area has a canvas cover, while the rear portion is a flat black metal coaming for the instrument panel.

The instrument panel, telescopic sight, and the aft end of the two fixed machine guns are visible in this photograph. Note the natural metal arming handles for the two guns.

A navigation or plotting board slid out from just below the lower instrument panel.

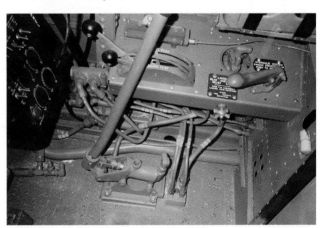

The right side of the pilot's cockpit can be seen in the photograph at left. The large black panel at the lower left is the electrical distribution panel. The green oxygen canister and regulator can be seen to the right in the same photograph. Note the levers on the side console. The one in the forward position with the black handle is the landing gear selector lever. The one with the black handle that is positioned to the rear is the landing flap selector lever, and the one positioned to the rear with the red handle is the dive flap selector handle. The large lever with the red cap, located between the seat and the console, is for the emergency hydraulic pump. The steel cable that can be seen at the top of the photograph is part of the hoisting cable used to lift the aircraft with a crane or suspend it from the overhead in a hangar bay. In the photograph at right, the seat has been removed to reveal the various lines beneath the right console. The emergency hydraulic pump is also visible. The engine-driven hydraulic pump is further aft on the console.

This is the left side of the pilot's cockpit. The large lever with the round black handle on the throttle quadrant is the blower control, while the one with the red handle is for the mixture. The throttle is shown in the forward position, and is the lever with the larger handle. The long lever extending aft from the throttle quadrant is the propeller pitch control. Below the throttle quadrant is another set of levers. The one on top with the red handle is the bomb release, and the one near the bottom is the bomb arming lever. The large chromate green lever near the floor is the arresting hook release lever. The black panel further aft has the fuel tank selector valve, and the trim control wheels located on it. The two large red handles are flare releases, and the smaller red "T" handle further aft on the console is the fire extinguisher pull. The red lever is for the wobble pump.

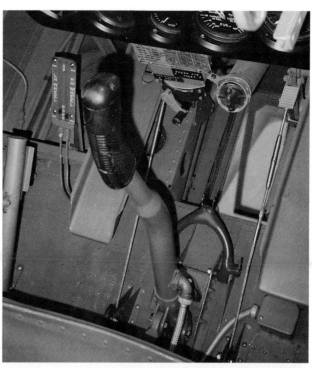

The control column is shown here. Mounted on the floor to the left of the handle is the landing gear position indicator. The tube with the black cap just below the instrument panel is the cockpit ventilation tube which brings in fresh air from a small circular hole in the leading edge of the left wing. The open window in the bottom of the fuselage can also be seen in this photograph.

This view looks directly down into the pilot's cockpit. The chutes for the pilot's feet can be seen, and between them is the hole in the cockpit floor that allows the pilot to look down through the window in the bottom of the fuselage. The control column and its linkage to the aft control column had been removed when this photograph was taken.

Here is a close-up of the right rudder pedal. (The left rudder pedal is identical.) Also note the natural metal chute in the background. This is the chute through which empty shell casings from the right fixed gun pass after being ejected. The shell casings exit the aircraft through a slot in the lower fuselage just forward of the wing root. There is a similar chute on the left side.

SBD-3 REAR COCKPIT DETAILS & COLORS

Electronic gear was placed in the area under the fixed portion of the canopy and beneath the two rear sliding parts of the canopy. On many SBD-5s and SBD-6s, a YAGI radar screen was located in the center of this area. Some, but by no means all, earlier versions of the Dauntless had a loop antenna located here. The black box to the right in this photograph is a homing adapter.

Most of the right side of the aft cockpit can be seen here. The microphone is on the console, and two confidential storage lockers with padlocks are visible at the forward end of the right side. The aft control column is installed in its socket, and the top of it can be seen at left.

This is the left side of the aft cockpit. The reel for the long wire trailing antenna can be seen to the right. When not in use, the control column for the rear cockpit was stored along this side as shown here. Note also the simple throttle located on this side of the rear cockpit. The cloth pouches contained flares for the signaling pistol which could be fired through the port located just above and slightly aft of the pouches.

More radio and electronic equipment, as well as some basic flying instruments, were situated at the forward end of the aft cockpit. This area was often covered by a dark gray, snap-in, canvas cover with flexible clear plastic windows to allow the crewman to see the instruments. In many cases this cover was removed during operational use. Note the socket for the removable aft control column at the center of the floor.

The aft end of the right side is shown here. The oxygen regulator for the aft cockpit takes up most of this corner. A portion of the ammunition storage box for the flexible guns is visible at right.

Here is a look at the flare pistol. The port through which it was fired is placed just in front of the muzzle of the pistol, and it can be seen in its proper position in the aircraft in the photograph at left. The pouch for the flares has also been placed on the table above the pistol.

Above left: SBD-1, SBD-2, and early SBD-3 variants were fitted with a single flexible .30-caliber machine gun in the rear cockpit as seen in this early SBD-3. This was standard through the Battle of Coral Sea in May 1942. Following that battle, official complaints, expressing the need for additional defensive firepower, resulted in the addition of a second gun as seen above. (National Archives)

Above right: A gunner loads ammunition into the dual flexible guns of an SBD-5 in late 1943. The dual guns were standard on all variants beginning with late production SBD-3s, and were retrofitted to early SBD-3s in the field. Note the radar scope located under the stowed canopy sections. Also visible is the port through which the flare pistol was fired. It is located partly within the red surround to the national insignia. (National Archives)

Left: With the guns, turret ring, and other equipment removed, the ammunition storage box for the dual rear guns is visible here. Note that the rollers for the ammunition belts are natural wood. There is a fire extinguisher located in the aft left corner of the rear cockpit. The rectangular hole in the floor was where all of the ammunition links and empty shell casings were dumped.

At left is a look into the aft end of the rear cockpit. Although the turret is now present, the guns are still not installed, and this provides a look at the four aircraft float lights located just aft of the ammunition box. These float lights had a wooden body and thin metal fins. A small light was mounted in the aft end of the body. A close-up of one of the float lights is shown at right. The nose was weighted so that the light in the aft end would be pointed up in the water.

ENGINE DETAILS & COLORS

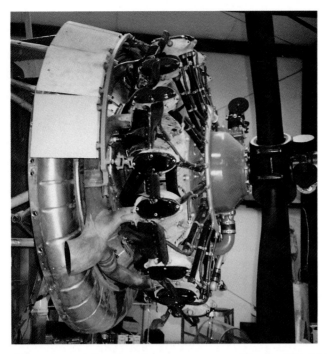
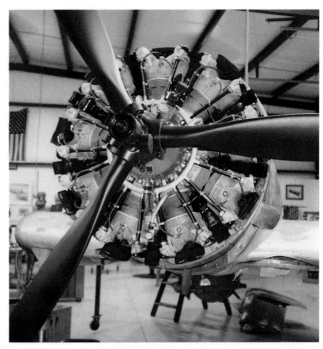

All versions of the Dauntless were powered by the Wright R-1820 single-row radial engine. Improved versions of this engine were used in the aircraft as subsequent variants of the SBD were produced, but there was relatively little change in the physical appearance of the engine. These two views show colors and details of the engine as installed during the restoration of SBD-3, 06508.

The aft end of the engine and its mounting frame are shown at left. At right is a look at the same area with additional equipment installed. The yellow cylinder at the bottom of this area is the oil cooler which received air through the scoop on the bottom of the aircraft just aft of the cowling. The tank at the top is the oil reservoir.

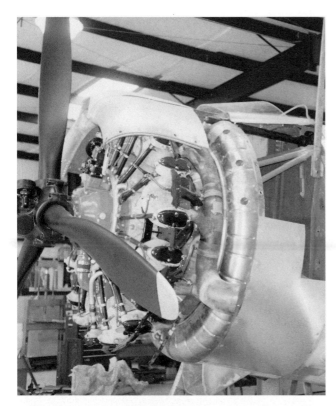

Details of the left side of the engine can be seen in these two photographs. At left, the top section of the cowling has been installed, while the three cowl flaps can be seen attached to the cowl ring in the view at right.

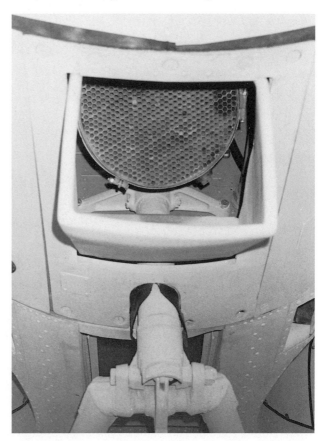

The aft end of the installed engine is seen here from the left side of the aircraft.

The oil cooler is visible inside the scoop under the aircraft. This scoop is located just forward of the bomb displacement gear. The oil cooler can be seen from the side in the bottom left photograph on the previous page.

OFFENSIVE ARMAMENT

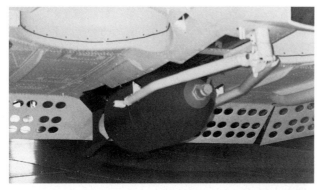

Explosive bombs were not the only ordnance carried by Dauntlesses. Here crewmen load a smoke tank on the centerline station. With it, the Dauntless could lay down a smoke screen to cover ships or other targets that might need to be concealed from the enemy. The exhaust of this Dauntless has a flame suppressor attached, and this was used to reduce the visibility of the flame during night operations. Also noteworthy is the fact that the plate has been removed from the right landing gear, thus revealing the spoked wheel at the extreme left in this photograph. SBDs used both a smooth tire (as illustrated on pages 30 and 31) and a treaded tire as shown here.

(National Archives)

Bombs up to the 1,600-pound size could be carried on the centerline station, however a 1,000-pound bomb, as shown in the top photo, was usually the largest size carried. The lower photograph shows a 500-pound bomb attached to the centerline rack, however the bomb displacement yoke has not yet been connected to the strap-on attachment points on the bomb's center section. Note the fuse and fuse wire on the bomb.

These two photographs show the area around the centerline station. At left is a photograph looking forward. Note that a metal plate could be attached over the lower fuselage window for aerodynamic purposes as seen here. However, this plate was seldom used in combat operations, and it was reportedly used more with A-24s than on SBDs. Another plate could also be attached to cover this entire area if bombs were not going to be carried. At right is a photograph taken from the front, and it clearly shows the window at the forward end of this area. The small doors on either side of the center of this area are in the closed position.

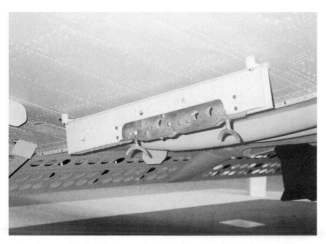 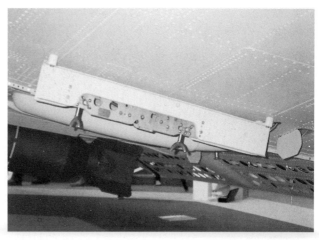

Bombs weighing up to 325 pounds could be carried on each of two bomb racks located under the wings. The 325-pound bomb that was carried was a depth bomb used against submarines. However, the most common bomb loaded on these stations appears to have been of the 100-pound size. On the SBD-5 and SBD-6, external fuel tanks could also be carried here. The bomb rack under the right wing is shown at left, while at right is the rack under the left wing. Note that the actual natural metal rack was often fitted inside a pylon that was painted the same color as the underside of the aircraft.

A 100-pound bomb is shown attached to the rack beneath the left wing. This photo shows the rack in place without its surrounding pylon. Demolition, incendiary, fragmentation bomb clusters, incendiary bomb clusters, and practice bombs were available for use on the Dauntless in the 100-pound size. This photograph originally appeared in a manual, hence the numbered callouts pointing to the pins and anti-sway braces on the rack.

(National Archives)

Here is a front view of the rack showing its alignment under the wing. Note that the rack is not perpendicular to the wing, but that it is offset so that it is aligned vertically.

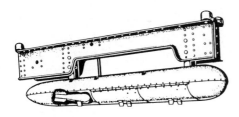 

Practice bomb dispensers could also be fitted to the wing stations, and these dispensers carried small practice bombs inside. The drawing at left shows the dispenser attached to a wing pylon, while the photograph at right shows it attached directly to the wing.

(Left, U. S. Navy; right, National Archives)

FIXED GUNS

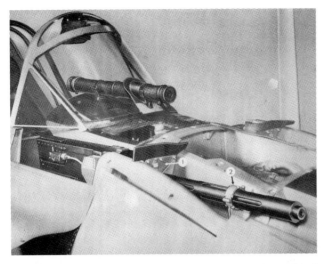

Above: All versions of the Dauntless had two fixed, forward-firing, .50 caliber machine guns which were fired by the pilot. This photograph was taken from the Pilot's Manual for the SBD-2, and it shows both of the two fixed guns in place. However, the manual also states that the left side gun was usually removed from the SBD-2 in order to save weight. This was done only on the SBD-2 and usually only during peacetime. Once the war started, the additional firepower of the second gun was more important than the weight advantage gained from deleting one of these guns. (National Archives)

Right: Regardless of the variant, ammunition for the two fixed guns was carried in boxes located on each side of the forward fuselage. A door, which was hinged at the bottom, was opened, then the ammunition box was slid out like a drawer for loading. Crewmen can be seen here loading the ammunition box for the right side gun. Note that the rounds were joined together by a belt of individual links which disintegrated as the rounds were fired. (National Archives)

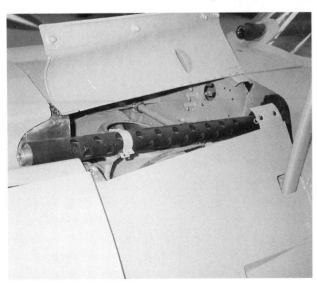

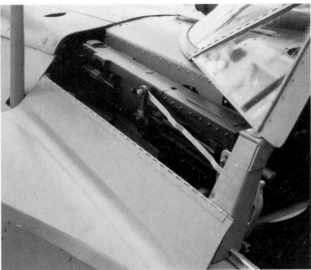

The left side .50-caliber gun in an SBD-3 is shown in these two photographs. In the view at right, note the metal arm extending from the gun's charging lever back to a handle inside the cockpit. This permitted the pilot to charge the guns manually. Also in the photo at right, the hinge for the side panel of the windscreen is visible in the upper right corner. This hinge allowed the outer panel of the windscreen to be moved up and out of the way whenever the guns were being installed or removed and when maintenance was being performed.

The aft end of the guns can be seen here along with the natural metal charging handles. The round counter for the right gun is visible just to the right of the charging handle, however the counter for the left gun has not been installed.

The natural metal chute for the expended shells is visible at the forward left corner of the pilot's cockpit. Another chute, which was a mirror image of this one, was located in the forward right corner for the other gun.

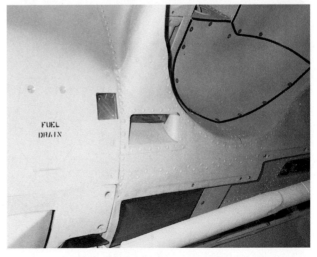

The openings through which the expended shells exited the aircraft are shown in these two photographs. In each case, the shells exited through the larger, rectangular-shaped opening next to the landing gear well. The individual ammunition links were discharged through chutes forward of the firewall, and they exited the aircraft through the smaller square-shaped opening just forward and slightly outboard of the chute for the shells. In the photo at right, the door for the fuel drain is also visible.

FLEXIBLE GUNS

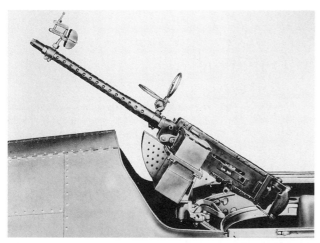

Above: On SBD-1s, SBD-2s, and early SBD-3s,   the flexible armament was a single .30-caliber machine gun as shown here. The ammunition box was on the side of the gun.   (National Archives)

Right: This photograph shows the single .30-caliber gun in the stowed position, but with the doors to the storage compartment open.   Additional ammunition boxes were carried in the rack below the aft end of the gun.
(National Archives)

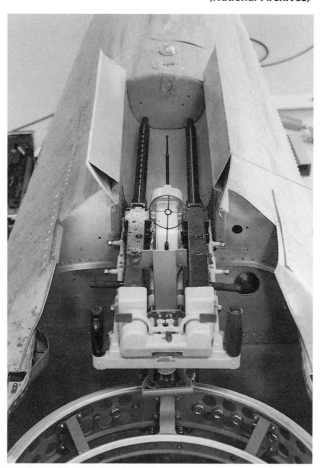

SBD-3s, which had been produced with single guns, were modified in the field to have a dual mount. Dual guns were the production standard for late SBD-3s and subsequent variants. The photograph at left was taken during restoration, and it reveals how the dual mount fits into the storage compartment. The sliding doors were not in place when this photo was taken. At right, the twin mount is shown from above, and the two sliding side doors that were added to aircraft with dual mounts are visible on either side of the original gun compartment doors.

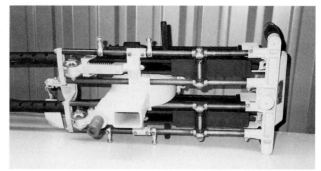

The twin mount was simply two .30-caliber machine guns that were joined together by a metal framework. A peg in the base of the framework mounted into the same hole in the gun ring that the previous single gun did. The framework was painted light gray, and the rods were natural metal. Ammunition was fed into the left gun from the left side in the conventional manner. The right gun's feed mechanism was reversed so that the rounds were fed in from the right side. Empty shell casings were discharged through the slots in the bottom of each gun, while the links were expended through the chute which is visible in the bottom of the framework. This underside view illustrates these features to good effect.

The complete twin mount is shown here to good effect. This photograph also provides a better look at the two sliding doors on either side of the gun storage compartment. The armor plate for the guns was often removed in the field as a weight-saving measure.

Here is a close-up view of the aft end of the framework showing the two handles and the thumb-actuated trigger mechanism. The triggers were painted red, and appear as dark rectangles just inside each handle in this photograph.

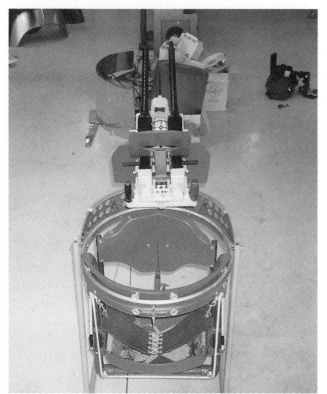

These two photographs show details of the gunner's seat, ring mount, and twin guns. At left is a view taken from behind the turret assembly, and at right is a close-up of the gunner's seat showing the seat belts. The web belt hanging above the seat forms the seat's back.

PILOT'S SEAT

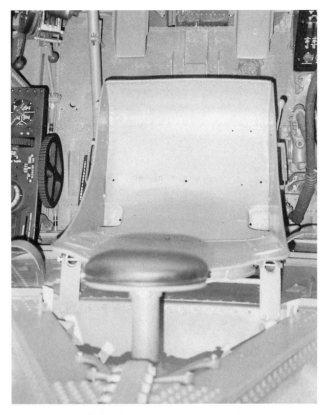

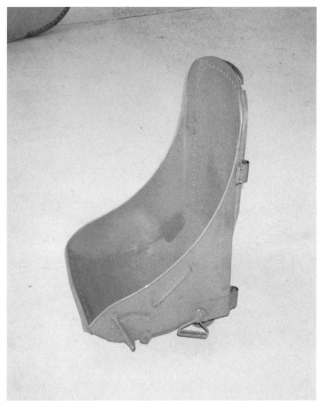

Details of the pilot's seat are illustrated in the four photographs on this page. At left is a top view of the seat installed in the aircraft but with the seat belts removed. Like the rest of the cockpit interior, the seat was painted chromate green. At right is a left side view of the pilot's seat.

The back of the seat is shown at left, while at right is a view of the bottom of the pilot's seat.

COWLING DETAILS

The only changes made to the forward lip of the cowling throughout the entire production run was related to the carburetor intake scoop at the top. On SBD-1s, this scoop was rather large, and on the SBD-2, -3, and -4, it was the size shown in the photograph at left. On SBD-5 and SBD-6 variants, there was no scoop as seen at right. The photograph at left also illustrates what the propeller hub on the SBD-1, -2, and -3 looked like with the spinner removed. In the photograph at right is the rounded hub of the propeller used on the SBD-4, -5, and -6.

One of the cowling latch handles is shown in the open position in this photograph.

A starter crank could be installed just aft of the cowling on the right side. The ventilation slot as seen on the SBD-3 and SBD-4 is visible as well.

FUSELAGE DETAILS

The spinner, cowling, forward fuselage, and canopy could all be protected from the elements with coverings.
(National Archives)

Small clips were located along the side of the fuselage, and the covering for the canopy was attached to these clips. One such clip can be seen in the very center of this photograph, and it is just above and aft of the forward fuselage step on the right side of the aircraft. The clips were only about two inches long, and therefore they usually do not show up in photographs.

Two steps were located on each side of the fuselage, with one being next to each of the two cockpits. The bottom of each step was coated with non-skid material.

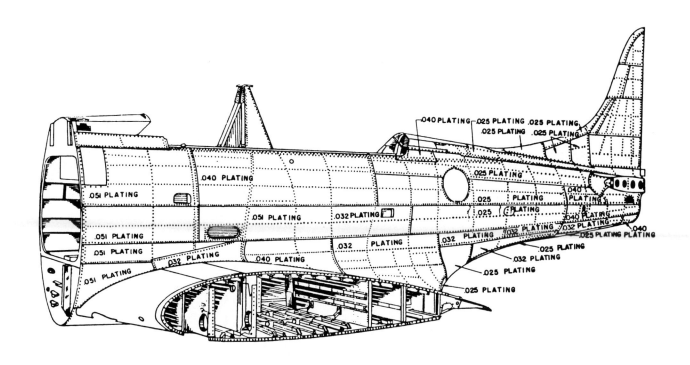

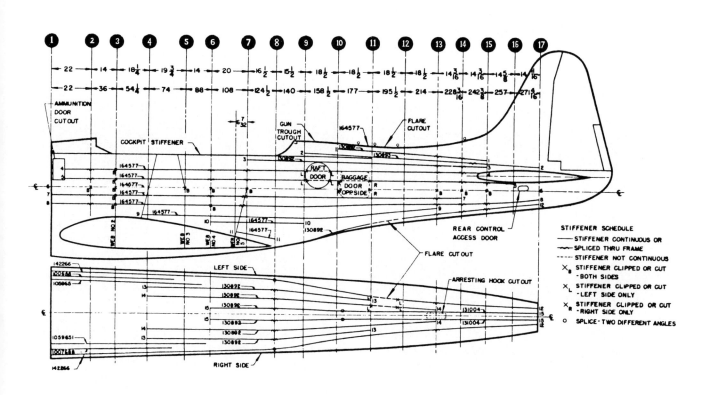

Details and dimensions of the fuselage are illustrated in these two official Navy drawings. (U. S. Navy)

The overturn structure was integral to the fuselage construction, and it prevented the heads of the crewmen from being crushed in the event the aircraft flipped over in an accident.

The mast for the radio antenna was made out of wood, although this is not commonly known, because it was painted the same as the exterior of the aircraft.

This close-up shows how the forward end of the wire antenna was attached to the mast. Note the white insulator between the antenna wire and the mast. A similar insulator was at the opposite end of the wire where it attached to the top of the vertical tail.

The antenna wire entered the aft cockpit at this position on the left side of the fuselage.

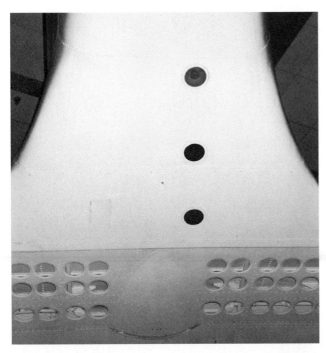

Three identification lights were located under the fuselage, just aft of the wing. The lights were red, green, and amber from front to rear.

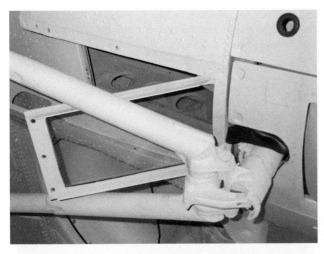

The window in the lower fuselage provided the pilot with the means to see whatever was directly below his aircraft. It could be opened so that it could be cleaned.

This view looks directly up though the window into the cockpit.

One of two flare tubes is shown inside the aft fuselage in this view that looks forward. The second identical flare tube is directly forward of this one, and therefore cannot be seen. Note the life raft tube in the background. These flare tubes jettisoned flares through two openings in the lower left fuselage. They were not present on A-24 Banshees. (National Archives)

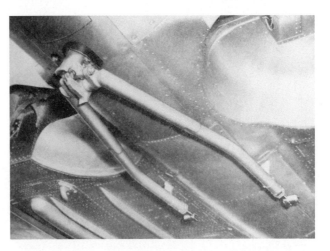

A metal plate could be fitted over the window as shown in this photograph. A second metal fairing, which is also visible here, could be placed over the recessed area where the centerline bomb was carried. Together, these two covers provided a smooth surface which reduced drag. However, they could only be used if no store was carried on the centerline station. (U. S. Navy)

On the left side of the fuselage was the door for the life raft container. The door was circular in shape, hinged at the bottom, and had a small triangular-shaped latch at the top. Just to the left of where the latch secured to the fuselage was a latch pin. The door was opened simply by pushing up on the pin to free the latch. Emergency rations were also stored with the raft. The raft was bright yellow.

On the spine of the fuselage, just aft of the doors for the gun storage compartment, were two lights. The forward one was green, although it appeared to be blue when not illuminated. The aft light had a teardrop shape and was clear.

On the right side of the fuselage was the door for the luggage compartment. It is shown closed in the photograph at left and open in the one at right. On the top of the door was a latch and a lock. The lock was very much like those found today on suitcases and brief cases, and it had a combination lock with three tumblers in the fuselage just above the opening. One might think that this was added to the aircraft by someone who obtained it from the military, but this is not the case. The lock is illustrated in the original manuals for the aircraft as published both by the Douglas Aircraft Company and the U. S. Navy.

WING DETAILS

The underside of the right wing is shown here. Many of the numerous access panels are in the open position.

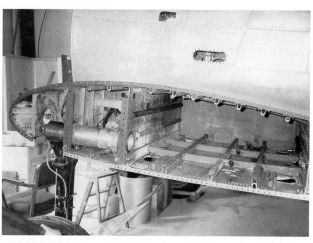

The interior of the left side of the center wing section is seen here without the fuel tank in place. How the main gear strut fits into the forward end of the wing's center section is also visible. Interior surfaces were painted chromate green.

This SBD-2 was recovered from Lake Michigan, and as this is being written, it is being restored at the National Museum of Naval Aviation. The inner right fuel tank can be seen still in place in the aircraft.

A photograph from a maintenance manual shows how the installed inner left fuel tank should look. (U. S. Navy)

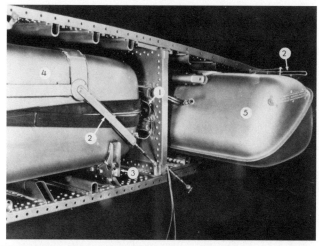

The SBD-1 had a unique fuel tank arrangement, with all fuel carried in the center wing section. On each side was a large 90-gallon tank shown here as item 4. A smaller auxiliary 15-gallon tank (item 5) was installed behind each main tank in the center wing section. Therefore, the total for both sides was 210 gallons. No fuel was carried in the outer wing sections of the SBD-1. (U. S. Navy)

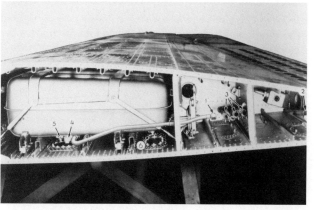

On all variants beginning with the SBD-2, the auxiliary fifteen-gallon tanks were deleted. Instead a 65-gallon tank was installed in each outer wing section as shown here. This increased fuel capacity to 310 gallons in the SBD-2. Beginning with the SBD-3, the four fuel tanks were the self sealing type, and fuel capacity was reduced to 254 gallons. Each tank in the center wing section held 75 gallons, while each of the tanks in the outer wing sections had a capacity of 52 gallons. (U. S. Navy)

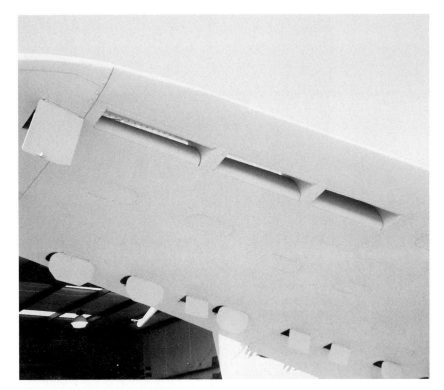

Three anti-stall slots were located near the tip of each wing. This view looks up through the slots on the right wing. These were often referred to as "mail box slots" because of their similarity in appearance to slots on mail boxes during that time period.

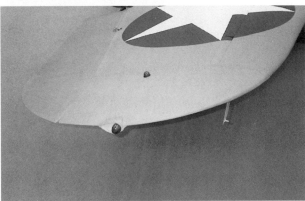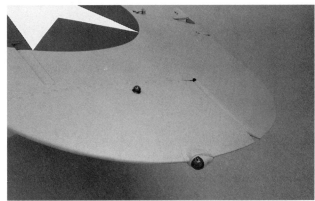

Both wing tips are shown in detail in these two photographs. Note the position lights on the very tips of the wings. The one on the left tip is red, and the one on the right is green. However, it has a blue color when it is not turned on. There are also two lights on the top of each wing near the tip, and both of these have the same blue color as the position light on the right wing tip. These lights are on top of the wings but not on the bottom.

These two photographs reveal the details of the ailerons. The ailerons extend from the dive flaps all the way to the tips of the wings. Note that only the left aileron has a trim tab. The mail box slots can also be seen in these views.

Some details, such as panel lines and rivet detail, are sometimes better illustrated in drawings rather than photographs. The four drawings on this page were all taken from U. S. Navy manuals.

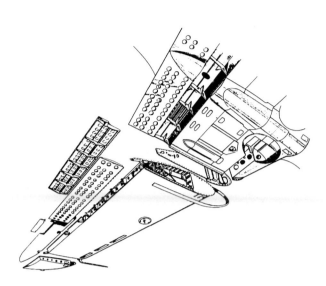

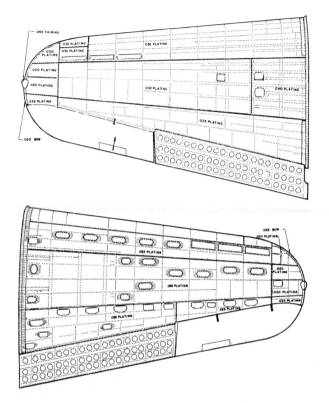

All major components of the wings are shown in this exploded view. They include the dive flaps, inner and outer wing sections, wing tip, pitot probe, landing light, aileron, aileron trim tab, and wing fairing.

The panels and rivet patterns for the wings are illustrated in these drawings. The upper drawing shows the top of the left wing, and the lower drawing depicts the bottom of the left wing. However, the retractable landing light is not shown. The panels and rivets on the right wing were a mirror image of what is shown here.

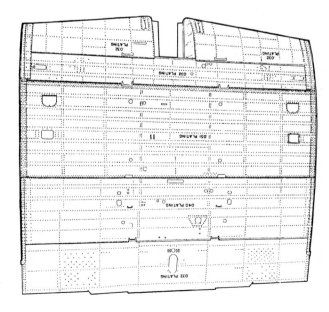

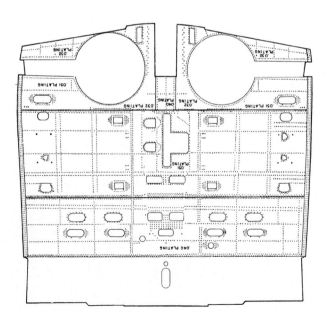

This is the top of the center wing section. Note the shape of the covers for the refueling points.

Here is a look at the underside of the center wing section. The fairings and catapult hooks have been deleted from this drawing which shows only the plating and panels.

On the leading edge of the left wing were the landing attitude indicator lights. These told the LSO if the aircraft was at the proper attitude for landing. The hole further inboard on the wing is where the ventilation air for the pilot's cockpit entered the aircraft. It was blown into the cockpit through a tube just below the main instrument panel. The fairing that covers the joint where the outer wing meets the center wing section was not in place when this photograph was taken.

Under the left wing was a retractable landing light. This was covered by a metal panel on some aircraft.

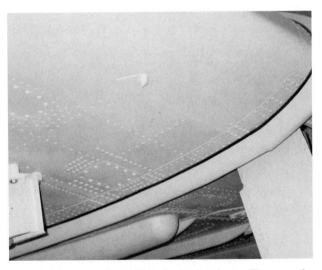

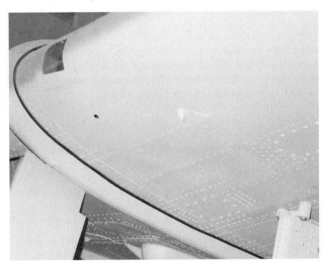

Jack points were located under both wings. They are the small protrusions forward of the wing racks a little more than half way out to the leading edge of the wing.

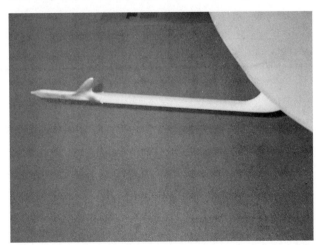

The pitot probe is shown at left. The tip is natural metal, and the rest of the probe is painted to match the exterior of the aircraft. At right is where the pitot probe enters the left wing tip. Just aft of it is a panel that can be opened easily to provide access to a tie-down ring.

The underside of the wing's center section is shown in these two views. Note the hooks for the catapult bridle, and the various fairings beneath the wing.

Two whip antennas can be seen beneath the center wing section of this Dauntless. The number and location of whip antennas varied from aircraft to aircraft.

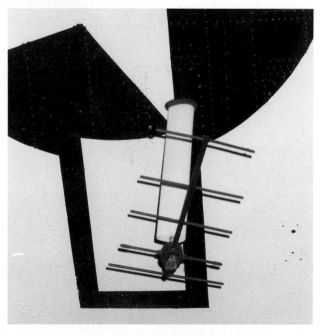

YAGI radar antennas were fitted beneath the wings of SBD-5 and SBD-6 variants. These were operated by the radio operator/gunner in the rear cockpit, and the scope was located under the fixed center portion of the canopy.

DIVE FLAP DETAILS

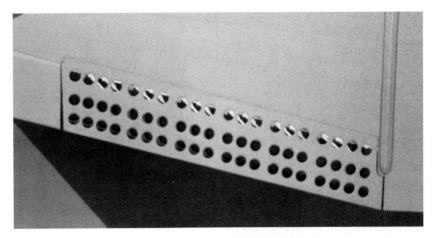

Here is a view of the left dive flaps in the closed position as taken from above and looking straight down. Note that the holes in the top flap do not line up with those in the lower flap.

The right dive flaps are shown here from above. Like the one above, this photograph was taken to illustrate how the holes do not line up. Also note that the white actuator arms for the dive flaps can be seen through the forward-most row of holes.

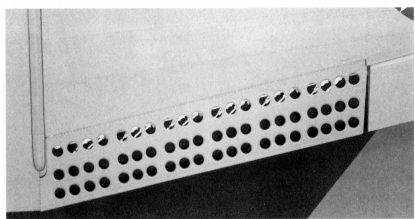

The right pair of dive flaps can be seen here in the open position. The interior of the flaps are painted insignia red. The actuating rods are shiny natural metal, and the arms between the rods and the flaps are white.

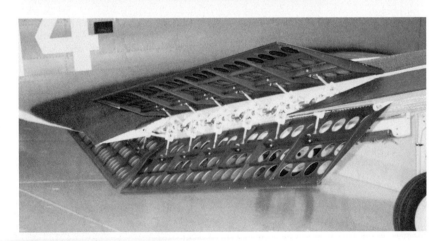

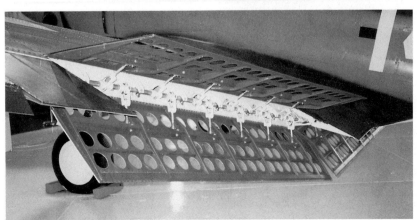

This photograph shows the open dive flaps on the left side.

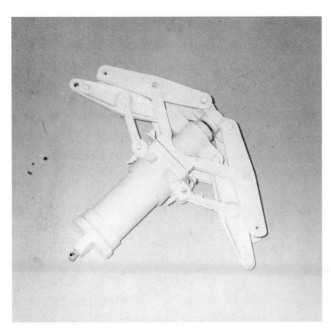

The actuator which operates all five sections of the dive flaps is shown here removed from the aircraft.

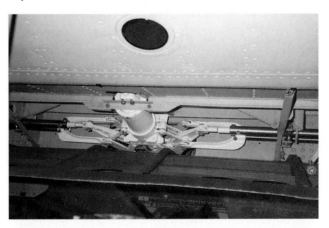

This is the same actuator seen above, but now it is installed in the aircraft. It is located at the center of the middle dive flap under the aircraft.

The inner edge of the upper dive flaps have a cutout where they meet the wing. This cutout allows the fairing for the wing joint to extend further aft.

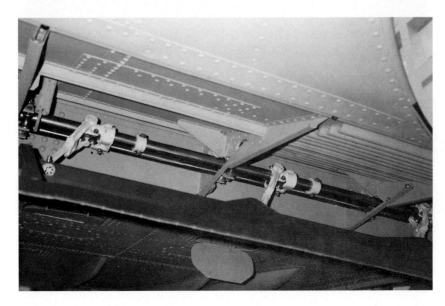

The actuating rods for the middle dive flap are illustrated in this photo. Again, they are bright natural metal, while the arms extending from the rods to the flaps are white.

TAIL DETAILS

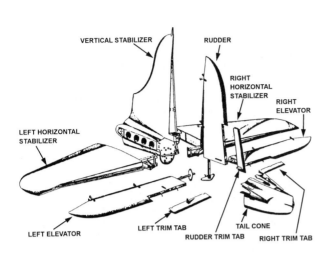

VERTICAL STABILIZER
RUDDER
RIGHT HORIZONTAL STABILIZER
RIGHT ELEVATOR
LEFT HORIZONTAL STABILIZER
LEFT ELEVATOR
LEFT TRIM TAB
RUDDER TRIM TAB
RIGHT TRIM TAB
TAIL CONE

This exploded drawing identifies all of the major components of the tail section.

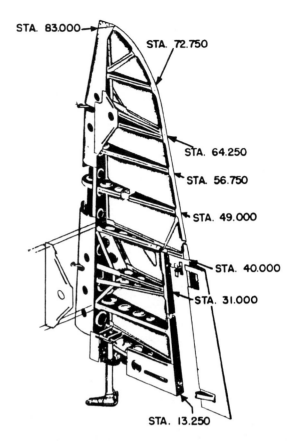

STA. 83.000
STA. 72.750
STA. 64.250
STA. 56.750
STA. 49.000
STA. 40.000
STA. 31.000
STA. 13.250

The framework for the fabric covered rudder is shown in this drawing.

Here is an overall view of the right side of the vertical tail and rudder.

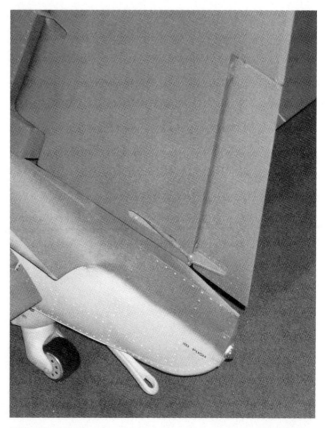

The trim tab for the rudder was operated through a linkage on the left side.

The tail cone is shown here. Note the clear light on the trailing edge. The arm extending down behind the tail wheel is a tow bar rather than a hold-back arm for the catapult system.

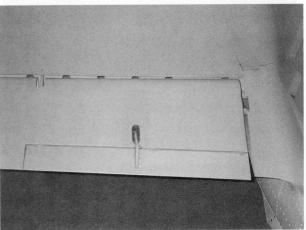

At left is an overall view of the left horizontal stabilizer and elevator. Both elevators had a trim tab, and the one on the left side was activated through a linkage on the top of the tab. These details can be seen in the photograph at right. Like the ailerons and rudder, the elevators were covered with fabric.

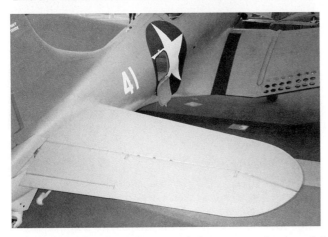

The right horizontal stabilizer and elevator are shown at left. At right is a close-up of the trim tab on the right elevator. In this case, the actuating linkage is on the underside of the tab.

ARRESTING HOOK DETAILS

The simple arresting hook used on all SBD variants is illustrated in these two photographs.

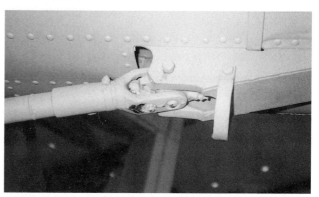

Details of the hook's actuator fairing can be seen here. It should be noted that although A-24s had the arresting hook removed, this fairing remained.

This underside view shows the hook from a different angle. Arresting hooks on Dauntlesses were sometimes highlighted with black stripes.

A rubber snubber was placed on the aft end of the fuselage just forward of the tail wheel. Its purpose was to keep the aft end of the arresting hook from vibrating against the fuselage.

MODELERS SECTION
KIT REVIEWS

1/144th SCALE KITS

Mitsuwa SBD-5, Kit Number 6

This Dauntless was packaged in a double kit with a Ju-87B Stuka dive bomber, and it is one of only two 1/144th scale kits of the Dauntless ever to be released. It most closely represents an SBD-5 or an SBD-6, and it includes two underwing fuel tanks. A bomb and yoke are provided for the centerline station.

Although small, the model comes with both a pitot probe and an arresting hook. Optional main landing gear parts are provided so that the model can be built in either a gear down or a flying gear-up condition. A complete propeller or a hub-only propeller with a clear plastic disc can be chosen depending on whether the model is to be displayed in flight or not.

The windscreen and canopy sections are represented by a single clear part, and there are no cockpit details inside the fuselage.

Decals include four large national insignia with the red disc at the center. Red and white stripes are provided for the rudder, and these decals are shown with a blue-gray over light gray scheme. However, neither these markings or this scheme is appropriate for an SBD-5 or -6.

This is arguably the better of the two SBDs that have been released in 1/144th scale, however it is no longer generally available. It can be found on collector's tables at swap meets, modeler's conventions, and at contests where it is valued in the $5.00 to $9.00 range. This same model has also been issued under the AHM label as kit number K418, and this issue is valued between $2.00 and $4.00.

Revell SBD-5, Kit Number H-1027

The one kit presently available of the Dauntless in 1/144th scale is from Revell. It has also been issued by Revells of Germany, Brasil, Mexico, and Japan.

Although this kit is accurate in outline, it does not have the detail of the Mitsuwa model covered above. Specifically, it lacks a pitot probe and the all-important arresting hook required for carrier landings. So if the modeler is not planning to build an A-24 Banshee, the hook should be made out of very fine wire. Wire can also be used to make a pitot probe. This was done quite easily when we built our review sample, and the two additions added considerably to its final appearance.

The model has a one-piece clear canopy, but no cockpit detail. This can be improved by using some plastic card to add at least a minimum of cockpit detailing. An overturn structure, forward instrument panel, and the decking between the two cockpits should be added.

The bomb for the centerline station is molded as part of the yoke, and the fins are in the + configuration instead of the proper X configuration. This was done as a result of molding considerations, and it results in a problem. When assembled, the bottom fin rests on the ground, and the aircraft cannot properly sit on its three-point landing gear. We cut the fins off, rotated them forty-five degrees, then reglued them to the bomb's body.

There are also wing pylons with 100-pound bombs molded on them. Again, the fins are in the + con-

The author used the Revell 1/144th scale kit to build this SBD-5. It represents a Dauntless from VB-16 aboard the USS LEXINGTON (CV-16) during late 1943.

figuration, but the bombs are so small that most modelers will not worry about this problem in such a small scale.

Fit is generally good except where the trailing edge of the wing meets the lower fuselage. Some filling and sanding will be required here.

The only decals that are provided are four national insignia that are the style with the bar added on each side but without the red surround. No specific aircraft is represented.

Overall, this is not a bad kit for 1/144th scale, but it can be improved with a little work and extra details.

1/120th SCALE KIT

Sanwa SBD Dauntless, Kit Number 190

This odd-scale kit has value only to collectors, and they list it in only the $3.00 to $6.00 price range. It is not a model that can be considered by a serious scale modeler.

1/96th SCALE KIT

Sanwa SBD Dauntless, Kit Number 1122

Here is another odd scale kit from Sanwa that has value only to collectors. Like the smaller Sanwa kit above, it is listed in the $3.00 to $6.00 price range. It was also released by UPC as kit number 7063 ($2.00 to $4.00), Nakamura as kit number 003 ($3.00 to $6.00), Okamoto as kit number 111 ($3.00 to $6.00), and Entex as kit number 8460D ($2.00 to $4.00).

1/72nd SCALE KITS

Airfix SBD Dauntless, Kit Numbers 252 and 02022-6

For many years, this was the best 1/72nd scale Dauntless available. It is better than the Aoshima/MRC and the Hawk/Testors models, but it is not as good as the newer Hasegawa kits. It suffers from a lack of detailing, and it has some serious accuracy problems.

The Airfix/MPC kit has been around for many years. For the most part, it is not as good as the Hasegawa 1/72nd scale kits, but it is better than the Aoshima/MRC or the Hawk/Testors models. The dive flaps are separate, so it is easy to drill out the holes and build them in the open position. The author used the MPC release to build this model of the aircraft shown on the front cover of this book.

The outline is generally correct, and it comes with some of the alternative parts to build an SBD-3 or a -5. These parts include different cowlings, one with the carburetor intake as used on the SBD-3, and one without the intake as used on the SBD-5. Both single and dual flexible gun mounts are provided for the rear cockpit. However, only the Hamilton Standard Hydromatic propeller used on the SBD-5 is included in the kit. It is relatively simple to modify this for an earlier variant, or the plastic disc that comes in the kit can be used to represent a spinning propeller. If this is done, only the hub will have to be modified for an earlier variant. Also, the kit does not take into account the fact that the ventilation slots on the sides of the fuselage changed from variant to variant. Finally, there is no telescopic sight provided for use with the earlier variants.

The cockpit interior is basic, and consists only of a floorboard, a seat for the pilot, a control column in the forward cockpit, and an instrument panel. There is also a cube which the gunner sits on, and this in no way represents the actual gun turret in the real aircraft. The rear gun (or guns) are mounted on a half-ring rather than a complete gun ring like the real thing. There is also no decking between the two cockpits, and this should certainly be added using plastic card. Airwaves makes a detailing set for the Dauntless in 1/72nd scale, and this set will improve the looks of the cockpit considerably.

The dive flaps are molded as part of the wings, and the holes are not opened up. Several sets of photoetched dive flaps are available in 1/72nd scale, and these can be used instead. For our review model, we simply drilled out the holes in the flaps before the wings were assembled, then we painted the inside of the flaps red. Before gluing the tops of the wings to the wing bottom, we also painted the outside of the flaps the appropriate color. This was done so that spraying on the colors after assembly would not cover the red inside the holes. Once the wings were assembled, the red color on the inside of the flaps showed through the holes in the opposite flap, and this was a nice effect.

The canopy consists of three different pieces, and the aft piece is simply to be left off if the rear cockpit is to be shown in the open position. The pilot's sliding canopy is to be deleted if the front cockpit is to be shown open. We decided it would be best to vacuform a new canopy so that all canopy sections could be represented.

The main gear wheels do not have the discs that cover the outer side of the wheel, and while these were deleted from a few aircraft in the field, we decided to make discs from thin plastic card. The landing gear doors are too thick, and new ones made from thinner plastic card will look better. There are no small braces between the gear strut and the door, so we made these from stretched sprue.

The bombs are rather crude, so we replaced the larger center bomb with one from the parts box and left the wing pylons empty. Bombs produced by True Details can also be used. There are stubs for the YAGI radar antennas to go under the wings, but the actual pronged antenna is missing. These can be obtained from a photoetched sheet from Airwaves.

Another major accuracy problem is the area where the centerline bomb fits on to the fuselage. The window is missing, and the recessed area where the bomb fits is totally wrong. It actually is just a faired area under the wing, with two little pins on which to locate the bomb. It would take a lot of work to get this area to look right.

Decals varied from one release to the next, but usually only basic markings were provided.

This same kit was issued five times under the MPC label. Kit 2-0101 had some deck crew figures added. Gunze Sangyo also issued this model as kit number X206. All issues bring less than $9.00 from collectors.

Aoshima SBD-5/-6, Kit Number 212

This kit is very crude, and simply cannot be considered by the scale modeler. The molding is very rough, and there is a lot of flash. Although the dive flaps are separate pieces, they really don't look like the real thing whether displayed open or closed.

There are no details in the cockpit, and the figures for the pilot and gunner don't look much like crewmen. The box art shows external fuel tanks under the wings, but these are not present in the kit. There are three bombs, and these are very poor. Likewise, the engine looks more like a toy than a R-1820. The decal sheet provides only four national insignia, and these are not proportioned properly.

This model was also released under the Entex label as kit number 8493D and the Farpro label as kit 110. MRC also issued the model as kit number 3001, while UPC sold it as kit number 8008. None of the issues are worth more than $6.00 to collectors, and they usually bring closer to $3.00.

Hasegawa SBD-3, -4, -5, & -6, Kit Numbers AP29, AP30, AP-31, & AP-32

These are not scaled down versions of the Hasegawa 1/48th scale Dauntlesses reviewed below, but they share some of the same problems and inaccuracies. Very few serious modelers will be happy with this kit built straight from the box.

The biggest problem is the dive flaps. The lower center section is a separate piece, but Hasegawa molded the four outer sections as part of the two upper wing sections. This is the worst possible choice. Clearly, it would have been best if all five sections of the dive flaps were molded as individual pieces, but if they were to be molded as part of the wings, then obviously they should have been separated with the top sections as part of the wing tops and the bottom sections as part of the wing bottom. But by molding them together, it makes it impossible for Hasegawa or the modeler to open the holes accurately. On the real aircraft, the holes in the top flaps are offset to varying degrees from the holes in the bottom flaps. By molding them together, even if the modeler drills out the small dimples used to represent these holes, they will line up rather than being offset. At least with the old Airfix kit, where the upper and lower sections were separate, the modeler could drill out the upper and lower holes and get a more accurate representation of the real thing. To adequately solve this problem, the modeler must turn to an etched metal after-market dive flap set that will replace those provided in the kit.

The "mail box" slots do not go all the way through the wings as they should. Hasegawa also put a trim tab on both ailerons. There should be one on the left aileron only. The lights on the tips of the wings are fine, but the small raised lights on the top of each wing tip are represented only by indented circles which are way too small in diameter.

Under the wings, the two small doors for the area where the centerline bomb attaches are missing. As with the 1/48th scale models, the clear window at the forward end of this area is represented only by scribed lines. Certainly, considering the high price of these kits, Hasegawa should have provided an opening with a clear piece to fit inside of it.

Another problem shared with the 1/48th scale kits is that Hasegawa scribed in the lock above the life raft compartment. Unfortunately, it belongs on the luggage compartment on the opposite side of the aircraft. Otherwise, the scribing is fine, but it represents only the panel lines. The very noticeable rivets of the Dauntless' skin are missing. The line that represents the separation between the rudder and the vertical tail is poor and does not represent the correct rounded leading edge of the rudder.

Another negative is the canopy. It is in three pieces that include the windscreen, the pilot's sliding portion, and the third piece with all three sections that cover the aft cockpit molded together. It cannot be built in the open position. To do so, the modeler will have to vacuform his own canopy or hope that an after-market company will produce one that will fit in the open position. At the price being charged for this model, one would think Hasegawa would have provided a closed canopy and a second one that could be assembled in the open position. Other companies have been doing this for over twenty-five years.

Cockpit detailing is very inaccurate. As with their 1/48th scale kits, Hasegawa has molded the cockpit floor as a solid piece. There should be a hole between the pilot's feet where he can look down through the window in the bottom of the fuselage. The pilot's feet go on rails that are located on each side of this opening. The rudder pedals move above these rails. There is absolutely no detailing on the sides of the pilot's cockpit. Not even the large consoles in the forward cockpit are provided, and the confidential storage lockers in the gunner's cockpit are missing. There is also no representation of the large radios at the forward end of the rear cockpit. What is provided is not always accurate. The control columns do not correctly represent those in the real aircraft, particularly in the aft cockpit.

To solve this problem, we recommend the True Details cockpit detailing set for this model. It is TD72461. Another good choice is the Jaguar Dauntless Detail Set

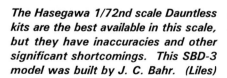

The Hasegawa 1/72nd scale Dauntless kits are the best available in this scale, but they have inaccuracies and other significant shortcomings. This SBD-3 model was built by J. C. Bahr. (Liles)

which is kit number 67201. But these add to the cost of an already expensive model, and Hasegawa should have provided this detailing in the kit.

The engine is one of the better features and is as well represented as one would expect to find in a 1/72nd scale kit. The cowling differs between the four issues, with the carburetor scoop being present for the SBD-3 and -4 versions and absent for the SBD-5 and -6 variants. The correct propeller and spinner for the SBD-3 is included in kit AP29, while all others have the proper Hamilton Standard propeller without the spinner.

Only the dual flex guns are provided. This is no problem except in the SBD-3 kit. Markings are provided for the ubiquitous 2-S-12 flown by Leppla and Liska at the Battle of Coral Sea. At that battle, the SBD-3s had only the single flexible guns. Although this point has been argued, the fact remains that only single guns were used at that battle by Scouting Two. Commander Dixon, the naval aviator who sent the famous "Scratch one flattop!" message at Coral Sea when the SHOHO was sunk, was the squadron commander for Scouting Two. His after-action report for that battle clearly states in the "Weapons Employed" block, "two .50-calibre fixed forward guns and one .30-calibre flexible gun" in his unit's SBD-3s at that time.

The landing gear is fair, but it is angled too far inward. The real thing does angle inward to a degree, but not as much as Hasegawa has molded it. A small brace between the strut and the door should be added from sprue. The main wheels leave a lot to be desired, and have noticeable ejector pin marks on them. They are best replaced with wheels from True Details.

The centerline bomb comes as four parts, and it is not the best engineering for fit either. This will prove challenging to fill and sand. Again, True Details can improve the kit with their resin bombs. Two 100-pound bombs are provided for the hardpoints under the wings, and these are fine as they come in the kit.

Overall fit is pretty good. The cowling will take a little work, and where the wings join the fuselage will require some filling and sanding. We recommend gluing the center section of the dive flaps in place during step two instead of step seven. This will help align the wing to the fuselage joints.

The outline of this kit is accurate, and it can be built into an acceptable model. But to really build it into the standards many modelers want today, a cockpit detailing set is needed, and the canopy should be vacuformed. Etched metal dive flaps should replace the ones that come in the kit.

J. C. Bahr contributed to this review.

Hawk/Testors SBD-5 and A-24, Various Kit Numbers

First released in the 1950s, this model has been issued no less than eight times by Hawk, and once by Testors. In each case the plastic remains the same, with changes only in the box art and decals. Hawk kits of the SBD usually had kit numbers that began with 611, and those for the A-24 models began with 612. The Testors issue is kit number 693.

Again, this is a very poor, inaccurate model that cannot be considered by the serious scale modeler. Four of the Hawk issues claimed that the kit was of an A-24, however no distinction was made between the A-24 Banshee and the SBD Dauntless. The A-24 kits all had the arresting hook and small tail wheel, and there were no instructions telling the modeler to remove the hook or modify the tail wheel.

There is no detailing to speak of. The "mail box" slots, the fairings under the center wing section, and even the wheel wells are represented only by panel lines. Inside the cockpit, two poorly molded pilot figures sit on two rectangular pieces of flat plastic. There is no cockpit detailing at all. The twin gun mount for the rear cockpit is very crude, and the guns are spaced too far apart. The canopy is one piece, and does not include the two pieces that go over the rear cockpit.

The bombs, engine, and landing gear are all very crude. There is no pitot probe and no pylons to go under the wings. Instead, the two smaller bombs fit right on the wing itself. Again, the area where the center bomb fits is totally wrong and does not have the correct recessed area.

When Testors released this kit, they included nice Scale-Master decals, and one of the choices is for Leppla and Liska's SBD-3 from the Battle of Coral Sea. However, the model represents an SBD-5 or SBD-6, so the decals are incorrect for this variant. The other option on the decal sheet is an SBD-5 from VS-37 in the Dark Gull Gray over white scheme.

Because so many details are missing or are represented only by panel lines, this kit would not even build up into a nice desk stand model. All Hawk issues of the kit bring between $6.00 to $10.00 from collectors except for kit number 611-50 which had Picture Gallery box art. It will go for $12.00 to $17.00 among collectors. Interestingly enough, kit 612-50, which had the Picture Gallery box for the A-24, lists only in the $6.00 to $10.00 range.

1/50th SCALE KIT

Imai SBD, Kit Number 807

Collector's guides show that Imai once released a Dauntless in this "off" scale. However, we have not been able to find one for review purposes, and no collector we have talked to can tell us anything about it. The model was also issued by Bandai as kit 8502. Neither issue is presently generally available, and because it is in an odd scale, we doubt that either of these two issues would be of interest to the scale modeler. The original Imai kit is listed in kit collector guides in the $4.00 to $8.00 price range, while the Bandai issue brings only $3.00 to $6.00.

1/48th SCALE KITS

Accurate Miniatures SBD-3 and SBD-5, Kit Numbers 3411 & 3412

At press time for this book, final test shots of these kits were made available to Detail & Scale for review, with release of the kits scheduled for early 1997. Certainly, there has been a long wait for these kits, but the results illustrated by the test shots are certainly well worth that wait. These are arguably the best and most detailed 1/48th scale aircraft models ever molded. The superb

The Accurate Miniatures 1/48th scale Dauntless models were received with excitement when they were exhibited at the 1996 IPMS/USA National Convention. They are far and away the best SBD kits in any scale.

detailing even includes the pilot's relief tube. Only the people who produce after-market detailing sets will be disappointed in these kits. Everything a modeler could want is provided.

The models have beautiful perforated dive flaps with the actuators included between them. The interior of the flaps are detailed. No expensive etched metal flap sets are required. From the engine to the demarcation between the rudder and the vertical tail, everything looks superb.

The cockpits are very well detailed, and the modeler has a choice of using decals for the instruments or painting and detailing the raised features. The hoist cable in the front cockpit is present, and there is even a map table that can be shown in the pulled-out position. A decal of the navigation wheel is provided to go on it. In the rear cockpit, full radio gear is included, and there is a choice of single or dual gun mounts. The flare pistol is in place, and the port through which it is fired is present.

The pilot's fixed guns are not just the breaches of the guns in the cockpit and the barrels at the other end on the cowling. Instead, the complete gun slips into place! These fixed guns and the flexible guns look in scale, being both delicate and accurate.

Surface scribing is engraved, delicate, and absolutely accurate. Even the combination lock for the luggage compartment is present and accurate, as are the tie downs for the protective cover for the canopies. The lower window, which Hasegawa left out, is included, and you can look into the front cockpit and see out the window just as you could on the real thing. This is because Accurate Miniatures provided the correct floor instead of the incorrect solid one as Hasegawa did.

There is a complete closed canopy, and as an option, stackable open canopies is also provided. If shown open, the air flow deflectors on the pilot's sliding canopy are in the actuated position.

The models have a positionable bomb displacement gear with a 1,000 or 500-pound bomb. There are also 100-pound bombs for the wing racks. The area where the

centerline bomb fits under the center section of the wing is accurate and has the appropriate doors. Both weighted and unweighted tires are also provided.

Appropriate cowlings are included based on the variant the model represents, and YAGI antennas are included for the SBD-5 variant.

Leppla and Liska's aircraft is represented in kit number 3411, and this is the first set of markings for this aircraft that are accurate. The SBD-5, kit number 3412, represents an aircraft from VB-16 during operations over Tarawa on 26 November, 1944.

Another nice feature of this kit is that historical information is provided about the model. In the SBD-3 kit, there is not only information about the aircraft, but a lot of material about the Battle of Coral Sea is also provided. There is a reproduction of a document which is a copy of the orders issued to the flight crews of VS-2 on the morning of 8 May 1942. These orders were typed aboard USS LEXINGTON (CV-2) and carried in Ensign Leppla and ARM-3c Liska's aircraft. The document lists all available aircraft and crews taking part in this operation from the group. Items like this increase the value of the kit and raise the level of the experience of modeling.

Hasegawa SBDs & A-24, Kit Numbers JT19, JT20, JT109, & JT119

These models were long awaited, and when they finally came out, the best that could be said for them was that they were a big disappointment. They suffer from numerous inaccuracies, and do not reflect the attention to detail which Hasegawa is usually known for.

The kits are cleanly molded and have scribed panel lines. But there is no representation of the raised rivets that are very prevalent and noticeable on the skin of the Dauntless.

The most disappointing feature concerns how the dive flaps are represented. They are molded as part of the wings, and are not even perforated. The instruction sheet shows that the dive flaps can be cut away from the wings by the modeler, then displayed in the open position. However, the interior of the brakes are not detailed, so this would detract from the appearance of the model. The one exception is Kit JT109 which is an SBD-3. Etched metal dive flaps are included in this issue, but it is very expensive.

The area where the centerline bomb goes is recessed, but it is inaccurate. The window just forward of the bomb is represented only by scribed panel lines. It would not have been very difficult to provide a flat clear rectangle for this window, and the price of the kit justifies this being done. So the modeler must open up the hole where the window goes and make a window from clear plastic to fit. The other option is to use kit part 24. This is the stream-lined fairing that was sometimes placed over this area when a bomb was not going to be carried on the center-line station. The forward end of this fairing would cover up the window, so it would not be seen from beneath the aircraft.

The cockpit has a number of details, but they are often inaccurate or incomplete. There is no hole in the pilot's floor through which to see out the window in the bottom of the fuselage. The cockpit ventilation tube is missing as well, as is the hole in the leading edge of the left wing which feeds air to it. Details on the sides of

The 1/48th scale Dauntless from Hasegawa is a disappointment. Note how the lack of peforated dive flaps detracts from the appearance of the model, particularly in this scale. It has numerous inaccuracies that will take a lot of work to correct. It also has fit problems in several places, an the worst of these is the canopy fit. In building this model, Jim Roeder had to leave the rear two canopy sections off in order to display the rear cockpit. Even trimming the rear canopy sections down will not allow them to fit in their stowed position under the fixed center section. There was no way to show the pilot's canopy in the open position using the parts in the kit. (Roeder)

both cockpits only resemble the real thing rather than accurately representing it.

The snap-in flexible cover for the forward end of the rear cockpit is a clear part that is to be painted except where the clear windows would be. This is unrealistic. The model has it set up so that this cover goes between the control column and the gunner, but this is backwards.

The position lights on the tops of each wing tip should be raised, however, they are represented by a circular recessed hole. There should be a brace between each main gear strut and the associated gear door, but these have been omitted from the kit.

As originally advertised, the primary aircraft kit JT19 was to represent was an aircraft from the USS RANGER during Operation Torch. However, before the kit was released, markings for Leppla and Liska's aircraft were added to the decal sheet. But that aircraft had the single flexible gun during the time frame for which these markings are appropriate. Hasegawa did not offer the option of both the single and dual flexible guns. Only the dual mount is included in the kit.

Some features are represented, but they are very poor. A case in point is where the rudder attaches to the vertical tail. The entire leading edge of the rudder was very rounded where it joined with the vertical stabilizer. This resulted in a very noticeable indented area between the vertical tail and the rudder. But Hasegawa represented this with only a panel line, and this is inexcusable. Even the old Monogram kit represents this feature much better.

The pylons that go under the wings are provided in the kit, but they do not include the bomb racks inside them, nor do they include any bombs. If the modeler can come up with some appropriate under-wing bombs, then he would have to build the bomb rack inside the pylon (at least the part that was visible) before installing them.

Some of the mistakes are quite small, but are noticeable nevertheless. A case in point is the lock that goes on the luggage compartment. It is not represented on the luggage compartment at all. This would be a nit pick if it was not for the fact that the lock is represented above the

door for the life raft compartment on the opposite side of the fuselage! It is only a small raised straight line, but it should be removed. It does not belong above the door for the life raft. A modeler can easily scribe in the appropriate latch and lock for the luggage compartment.

Fit is not up to the standards that we have come to expect from Hasegawa, and the biggest problem area is the canopy. As provided in the kit, the canopies cannot be displayed in the open position, although one might believe this was possible due to the fact that the windscreen and canopies come as five separate pieces. But even if built in the closed position, there will be fit problems. The air flow deflectors are not represented on the pilot's sliding canopy section. Squadron has a clear vacuformed canopy in 1/48th scale, and it is item number SQ9541. Although originally designed for the Monogram kit, it might prove helpful with these kits if the modeler wants to display the canopy sections in the open position.

There are inaccuracies on the decal sheet in kit JT19 as well. The instructions show that decals 21 or 22 can go on the tail of both Leppla and Liska's SBD-3 and the aircraft from VS-41. These two decals are the Bureau Numbers of the aircraft, and they are 6497 and 6674. They can only apply to one aircraft, not to both. But neither of these Bureau Numbers is correct for Leppla and Liska's SBD-3, which was BuNo. 4647. Further, a photograph of the aircraft from VS-41 that this kit represents shows that it was in fact an SBD-4, not an SBD-3. But it is possible that at one time, an SBD-3 did carry the number 41-S-16.

Hasegawa's second release of this model is an SBD-4 and this is kit number JT20. This issue comes with a Hamilton Standard Hydromatic propeller which is correct for the -4 version. Kit JT109 is another SBD-3, and it has the etched metal dive flaps mentioned above. Kit number JT119 is an A-24A Banshee.

Overall we are very disappointed with these kits, and we cannot recommend them. A modeler could take the time to correct all of the inaccuracies, and if so, a nice model could be built using it. However, we believe the

Accurate Miniatures kits are a far better choice.

Monogram SBD, Various Kit Numbers

Dating back over thirty years, this kit represented the state of the art in modeling around 1960. It had a number of toy-like operating features, to include movable dive brakes, a dropable bomb, retracting main gear, rolling wheels, and a movable gun. These working parts detracted from the accuracy of the model, but for years this was the only 1/48th scale Dauntless on the market.

Some diorama accessories were included in the kit, and these consisted of an LSO with paddles, a wind-over-the-deck shield, an aircraft mechanic, and a bomb dolly.

The model most closely represented an SBD-4, because it had the carburetor scoop on the cowling, the telescopic sight, and the Hamilion Standard Hydromatic propeller. But it could be easily converted to a -2 or -3. Only the single flexible gun was provided, and that is not correct for a -4.

The old Monogram 1/48th scale kit was built by the author to represent the SBD-3 crewed by Ensign J. A. Leppla and his gunner, John Liska, during the Battle of Coral Sea in May 1942.

A lot of work could turn this into a respectable model, but with better kits now available, it is best left to the collectors. Kits PA 54-149 and PA 54-150 now bring $18.00 to $24.00 from collectors. A second issue as PA 54-150 is valued at $15.00 to $20.00, while the Confederate Air Force issue as kit number 5212 brings only $10.00 to $15.00. Kit 6830 is listed in collector's guides in the $5.00 to $9.00 range. Nichimo also released this

model as kit number 5-4805, and it has a value to collectors between $12.00 and $17.00.

1/32nd SCALE KIT

Matchbox SBD-5, Kit Number PK-503

This is not one of the better 1/32nd scale kits available, and it takes a lot of work to make it look like an accurate Dauntless. Details that might be overlooked in 1/72nd scale are missing, and in 1/32nd scale their absence is noticeable.

The model is molded in blue, white, and clear plastic and features heavy raised panel lines. Cockpit details are rudimentary and very inaccurate. In this large scale, the cockpit will have to be rebuilt from scratch to look correct. The mount for the flexible guns is a half ring rather than being the correct full ring. There are no details on the sides of the rear cockpit, nor is there any representation of the radio gear under the center section of the canopy.

The windscreen and canopy pieces are thick, and the framework is not entirely accurate. There is no representation of the air flow deflectors on the pilot's sliding canopy section. The window in the lower fuselage is not represented at all.

As with most other kits, the area where the centerline bomb attaches to the center wing section is totally incorrect. It is recessed, but it is in the shape of a bomb. The dive flaps are molded separate from the wings, and the holes are open and correct in number.

The propeller is too small in diameter, and other details, such as the landing gear, bomb displacement gear, and the underwing bomb racks, are crude. No bombs or external tanks are provided to go on them. The lip of the cowling is also incorrect in shape. The light under the left wing is missing as are the approach indicator lights and the hole for cockpit ventilation in the leading edge of the left wing. Also omitted from the kit are the formation lights on the tops of the wing tips, at the very tips of the wings, on the spine of the aircraft, and on the tail cone. Likewise, the identification lights under the fuselage have not been represented. Another missing feature is the rear tow bar which would be very noticeable in this scale. The steps in the side of the fuselage are very poorly represented, and are not deep enough. The side doors for the flexible gun compartment are not represented at all.

The shape of the kit is basically correct, but in order to build a nice model, almost every part will have to be

Clyde Mills did an excellent job reworking the old Matchbox 1/32nd scale Dauntless in order to build this award winning SBD-5. The kit is quite crude, and suffers from a number of significant inaccuracies.

reworked. Many parts will have to be replaced completely, and others that are missing will have to be made from scratch.

Decals include a Dauntless from VMSB-231. This is a Marine land-based aircraft, and it should have the larger pneumatic tail wheel, a feature that is not included in the kit. Markings are also provided for an aircraft from Number 25 Squadron of the New Zealand Air Force and for a French A-24B. Both of these aircraft should also be fitted with the pneumatic tail wheel.

Overall, this is a poor kit, but it is the only Dauntless available in 1/32nd scale. The same model was also released under the AMT label as kit number 7203. It is now listed in the $18.00 to $24.00 range by collectors. Hopefully, another manufacturer will soon release a state-of-the-art Dauntless in this scale.

Clyde Mills contributed to this review.

ACCESSORIES

Airkit Cockpit Placard

This thin clear sheet of plastic has the main instrument panel and the electric distribution panel printed on it in black. This gives the instruments the appearance of having glass faces. It is available only in 1/72nd scale.

Airwaves Dauntless Dive Flaps

This photoetched metal sheet not only has all of the dive brakes with the appropriate holes, it also provides the YAGI antennas and the main landing gear doors for 1/72nd scale kits. A tiny part is also included that is the short mast at the top of the vertical stabilizer. This is where the aft end of the wire antenna is attached to the aircraft. The instructions say that this sheet of photoetched parts was designed for the Hawk/Testors kits, but that it will fit the Airfix/MPC model as well. We checked the fit on our MPC model, and they do fit.

Airwaves Dauntless Detail Set

A second photoetched metal set from Airwaves provides cockpit details for the SBD in 1/72nd scale. Included is a single piece for the floor and side walls. Smaller detailing pieces include the pilot's armor and bulkhead, throttles, forward instrument panel, pilot's seat, harness, and buckles, and the chutes for the pilot's feet under the rudder pedals. The snap-in cover for the rear cockpit is also provided. Although the modeler will still be left to do a lot of detailing on his own, this is a good place to start in order to improve the cockpit of any 1/72nd scale Dauntless.

Falcon Vacuformed Canopies

One of several 1/72nd scale canopies available from Falcon is for the SBD Dauntless. It is also available in 1/48th scale.

Fotocut Dauntless Dive Flaps

In addition to Airwaves, Fotocut also makes dive flaps for the Dauntless in 1/72nd scale. They also have a 1/48th scale set of dive flaps as well.

Jaguar Dauntless Detail Set, Kit number 67201

Jaguar makes a detailing set for 1/72nd scale Dauntlesses. It has cockpit details as well as control surfaces for the tail section.

Medalion Models SBD Detail Set

Consisting of twenty-seven parts, this excellent plastic and white metal set was designed for the Monogram Dauntless in 1/48th scale. Although the release of new SBD kits has eliminated the necessity of using the old Monogram kit, this detailing set is truly worth a look. It has a cockpit floor, bulkheads, cockpit sides, throttles, bomb release handles, fuselage overturn structure, gun turret and rings, seats, ammunition box, the pouch for the flares, and much more. One problem is the fact that it provides only the single flexible gun, but it has the large ammunition box used with the dual gun mount. However, this excellent set has been discontinued, so anyone who wants one needs to look for it on collector's tables at conventions, contests, and swap meets.

Missing Link Models SBD-5 Conversion Kit

Missing Link issued this kit to convert the Monogram Dauntless to an SBD-5. It included a cowling without the carburetor scoop, forward fuselage, and the dual flexible gun mount as used on the SBD-5 and -6.

True Details Cockpit Set, Item Number TD72461

True Details has produced a nice cockpit detailing set for the Hasegawa SBD kits in 1/72nd scale. This resin set is quite an improvement over the poorly detailed and inaccurate cockpits that come in the basic Hasegawa kits. Considering its very reasonable price, it is a very worthwhile addition to any of these models.

True Details Dauntless Wheel Sets

Two main gear wheels with smooth tread are included in these resin sets for 1/72nd and 1/48th scale Dauntlesses. The tires are flattened and slightly bulged to represent the effect of weight on the aircraft.

Tom's Modelworks Naval Aircraft WW-II Detail Set

This small photoetched metal set provides detailing parts for the single and dual flexible gun mount, bomb, engine, and YAGI radar in 1/48th scale. The YAGI radar antennas appear to be a little small for this scale, but all other parts look correct. Parts for the twin gun mount include the side and top armor, machine gun belts, gun ring, sights, and handles. All parts necessary to build a gun ring are provided, and there is a spinner type fuse for the bomb. Miscellaneous instrument bezels are included for the instrument panel, and wire harnesses are provided for the engine. This very nice set will help dress up any 1/48th scale Dauntless as well as other World War II naval aircraft.

Waldron Model Products SBD Cockpit Placards

Waldron Model Products makes two sets of their excellent cockpit placards for the Dauntless. One is in 1/48th scale, and the other is in 1/32nd scale. These can be found in better hobby shops, in various mail order houses, or by writing directly to Waldron Model Products at P. O. Box 431, Merlin, Oregon 97532.